ANTHONY CROWLEY is a multi award-winning playwright, composer, director, designer, dramaturge and educator. Musicals include: *The Journey Girl*, *Tribe*, *Super-freaks*, *Nathaniel Storm*, *The Villain Of Flowers* and *The Wild Blue*. He is the recipient of several awards including: the Wal Cherry Play Of The Year Award, the Malcolm Robertson Prize for Drama, the Sumner Locke Elliott—New Dramatists Award, an R.E. Ross Trust Award, an Australian Musical Foundation Grant, an Opera Australia Young Artists Residency, the Pratt Prize For Musical Theatre and the Victorian Premier's Literary Award for Best Music Theatre Script.

MOTOR-MOUTH LOVES SUCK-FACE
An Apocalyptic Musical

ANTHONY CROWLEY

CURRENCY PRESS
The performing arts publisher

CURRENCY PLAYS

First published in 2018
by Currency Press Pty Ltd,
PO Box 2287, Strawberry Hills, NSW, 2012, Australia
enquiries@currency.com.au
www.currency.com.au

This revised edition first published in 2019.

Typeset by Dean Nottle for Currency Press.
Cover photograph by Siena Stone, Art Direction by Anthony Crowley.

Contents

Currency Press acknowledges the Traditional Owners of the Country on which we live and work. We pay our respects to all Aboriginal and Torres Strait Islander Elders, past and present.

INTRODUCTION

Motor-mouth Loves Suck-face is a musical comedy about the end of the world. On the surface it's about two geeks in love, trying to lose their virginity before the world implodes in a zombie apocalypse. At a deeper level it also pits idealism against nihilism, explores the tension between parents and children—and the existential journey to find meaning and purpose, either through love or some form of altruism. And, of course it's also about rebellion. Our restless yearning for a better world and the horrors we must all confront on a daily basis.

In terms of style, *Motor-mouth Loves Suck-face* breaks with the narrative structure used by many contemporary musicals by telling the story back—and forth—dropping ambiguous clues through time and space, for the audience to connect the dots. It is set in a non-naturalistic world where several realities can exist simultaneously. It drops in and out of internal psychological moments and action, and breaks the fourth wall—using music and rhythmic, heightened dialogue—to accentuate these shifts.

Thematically, it immerses a cast of recognizable characters in a lurid world that becomes a funny, imaginative metaphor for the horror of the real world. The most obvious issue it raises is global warming and the environmental inheritance we're leaving young people, but the show uses the context of climate change as a springboard to wider issues.

Theatrically it employs a Brechtian approach to zombies, teenage love, desire and Armageddon, utilizing music, dance, comedy, heightened characters and ludicrous plot elements to depict a world that is imploding in a vortex of hypocrisy and cynicism. It explores the redemptive power—and cruelty—of love and desire, and musical comedy sex, with humour and wit that never becomes uncomfortable, or graphic—thanks to the language it employs, the fun it exudes and the musical world in which it exists.

The text integrates spoken word with poetry and lyric. It utilizes rhyme for visceral, comedic and dramatic effect. As the work developed the creative team experimented with zombie movement and how to adapt this into dance. We developed a physical language based on our investigations. The score balances musical comedy with modern pop, creating irony through pastiche. The play is about choices, about standing for something, even when you're not sure what that something is yet. By allowing the audience to laugh and groove—and revel in its silliness—*Motor-mouth Loves Suck-face* opens the door to an important and at times difficult conversation. But like a great dinner guest, it breaks the ice and enables that conversation to take place in the context of experimental musical comedy.

In production, the set and costume design was simple and allowed the actors and the director to constantly 'endow' and reinvent the space to create various settings, situations and explore different relationships. The set allowed the actors space and opportunity to play; the use of 'poor theatre' invited the audience to use their imagination from the very first zombie death. The creative team deliberately used vivid colours to heighten the world, and costuming that targeted the vividness and independence of young fashion, as well as a smatter of nostalgia. We were not trying to capture reality, but we wanted an audience to identify with the characters. The set used three icons of an affluent home, which the actors endowed—a swimming pool, a tennis court and a croquet lawn.

The script of *Motor-mouth Loves Suck-face* started development in 2007 where it began life as a play. The first draft was written after several weeks investigating the issues facing young people—and the challenges they found compelling, which included climate change, activism, agency to manifest change, injustice and relationships that give meaning to life. The play was then performed at St St. Martins Youth Arts Centre.

In 2015 the work was adapted into a first draft musical and work-shopped by Federation University Arts Academy students as part of their second year studies. In 2016 a workshop production was staged at Chapel off Chapel to gain audience insight—as well as dramaturgical feedback from industry professionals. A further draft of the work was then undertaken and the production at La Mama Courthouse in 2018 was the result of all that development and commitment. Many of the cast and creative team stayed with the show through its various stages of development and production, including from the very first performance.

I would like to thank Liz Jones, the staff of La Mama and the VCAA for their support of Australian theatre. I also want to express my deep gratitude to Currency Press as well as the City of Stonnington, Chapel Off Chapel, Federation University Arts Academy, the respective casts of the 2015 and 2016 development seasons, David Wynen, Christian Leavesley, Jolyon James, Petra Kalive, Luke Gallagher, Abi Richardson, Danielle Carter, the Crowley family, members of the 2007 St. Martins Youth Arts Centre Foundation Ensemble, and everyone who donated to our 2016 Pozible campaign, for their generous support and advice.

Anthony Crowley
October 2019

Following a workshop production at Federation University's Arts Academy in 2015, *Motor-mouth Loves Suck-face: An Apocalyptic Musical* was first presented in Chapel Off Chapel's Loft Theatre, Melbourne, on 5 October 2016 with the following cast:

ZOMBIE BOY	Lachlan Hamill
BLASKO TUPPER	Olivia Charalambous
MOTOR-MOUTH	Brenton Gardiner
SUCK-FACE	Sophie Jackson
PENELOPE TUPPER	Danielle Matthews
CHRISTOPHER TUPPER	Harley Morrison
SARAH TITAN	Luisa Scrofani
ZACK STELLAR	Thomas Bradford
PIPER LANE	Ashleigh Kreveld
RAINBOW PHOENIX	Safiye Vurdu
TIFFANY FLAKE	Jessica Harris
HILARY STUCKLE	Belinda Jenkin
HUGO DUDE	Elias Jabbour
TANK RAMONE	Nicole Kaminski

Director and Designer, Anthony Crowley
Lighting Designers, Rob Sowinski and Bryn Cullen
Sound Designer, LSS Productions
Musical Director, Mark Jones
Choreographer, Elenor Smith Adams
Assistant Director, Siena Stone
Stage Manager, Hayley Fox
Assistant Stage Manager, Ella Crowley
Sound Operator, Dana Samuel
Production Manager, Liz Verber

CHARACTERS

ZOMBIE BOY

BLASKO TUPPER, Icelandic accent

PENELOPE TUPPER, British accent, Blasko's mother

CHRISTOPHER TUPPER, French accent, Blasko's father

MOTOR-MOUTH

SUCK-FACE

HILARY STUCKLE

SARAH TITAN

ZACK STELLAR

HUGO DUDE

TANK RAMONE

TIFFANY FLAKE

SETTING

The time is now. A mansion in an affluent Australian suburb. A public school in a poor Australian suburb. A cosmic wormhole.

AUTHOR'S NOTE

The pop culture references should be updated from time to time.

ACT ONE

SCENE ONE

The well-manicured garden of a wealthy mansion. The remains of a lavish teenage party. The sound of a bomb exploding. ZOMBIE BOY *rises from the dead. He is joined by other* ZOMBIES—*performing a broken-limbed, rotting-flesh song and dance.*

SONG: 'RATHER BE A ZOMBIE'

ZOMBIE BOY: [*singing*] 'If Armageddon
          Is where we're headin'
          I know that I would rather die
          Being a zombie
          I'd rather be a zombie
          If every nation's annihilation
          And judgment day is on the way
          I'd rather be a zombie
          I'll be zombie

          If a solar flare from outer space
          Is gonna
          Incinerate the human race
          I'd rather
          Eat your liver than look up and see
          The end of days
          Raining down on me

          If the prediction is our extinction
          Before we fry it's time to try
          Being a zombie—eh, eh
          Apocalyptic's no longer cryptic
          The end is nigh—don't ask me why
          I'm just a zombie, I'll be zombie

          As a zombie you don't feel the pain

If you can be distracted eating someone's brain
So what if Armageddon is a fricassee
It's ninety-nine percent fat free
If where we're headin' is Armageddon
Oh, can't you see, I'd rather be
I'd rather be, I'd rather be, I'd rather be

BLASKO TUPPER *enters and kills* ZOMBIE BOY *with a chainsaw. He springs back to life to finish the song.*

A zombie'

ZOMBIE BOY *is cut down with the chainsaw again.*

BLASKO: [*to the audience, spoken with an Icelandic accent*] Shut up and listen. In exactly one minute and fifty-three seconds a solar flare will strike the earth—setting off a chain reaction incinerating every living creature on the face of the planet. But that's not important right now—what's important is this. *This* precious moment just before the end, because if you can understand this, if by some miracle clarity wedges its sweet toe through the dark door of apathy, then maybe, just maybe there's hope for us all in this knee-deep, existential sludge pile we so loosely refer to as *life*. Actually, now that I think about it—that's not important either. No, no, no, no, no— [*making a phone call*] what's important is the phone call I almost forgot to make to the only two people in the entire multiverse who can save the planet … and it's gone straight to message bank. Motor-mouth, Suck-face, listen carefully, I'm calling from another dimension and my credit is running out. Moments ago I transmitted a top secret text message containing a list of items. When the time comes you must deliver these items to me after locating the brain in a pickle jar next to the bomb. We then have until the last polar bear dies at midnight to send Professor Pluto's consciousness through the wormhole and save the planet in the other dimension. Just to be clear, the dimension you will be saving is not your own dimension but the dimension beyond your dimension … which is actually the dimension beyond, *beyond*, the dimension I am calling from. Which is why you must tell the 'me' in your dimension the truth, because—to be perfectly honest—if the 'me' in your dimension is anything like the 'me' in this dimension she will be very one dimensional— *But*—you tell *your* 'me' from *this* 'me' that whatever kills 'me' in one dimension only makes me stronger in another.

> ZOMBIE BOY *comes back to life.* BLASKO *kills him again with the chainsaw.*

I am of course referring to the 'me' in *your* dimension not the 'me' in *this* dimension, who along with this message and rest of the planet, will self-destruct in exactly ten seconds. [*To the audience*] Translation? It all started with a party. The party to end all parties. My name is Blasko Tupper.

> *She pauses before hitting the hash key.*

Prepare to die.

> *She hits the hash key—boom!*
>
> *The sound of an apocalyptic explosion.*

SCENE TWO

The party. Several hours earlier—same dimension. ZOMBIE BOY *rises from the dead. The other* ZOMBIES *reanimate as* TEENAGERS. *A neon sign reads 'THE END'. A toy polar bear sits on a tiny iceberg floating in a kids' sea-shell swimming pool.*

SONG: 'MY POLAR BEAR'

ZOMBIE BOY: [*singing*] 'Polar bear floats on her iceberg
    White as snow, out on the sea
    Melting close to the equator
    Drifting far away from me
    Will you ever return now we're so far apart?
    Do you trust me to make it right
    After breaking your heart?
    Polar bear'
ALL: 'Polar bear'
ZOMBIE BOY: 'Don't you leave, oh polar bear'
ALL: 'Polar bear'
ZOMBIE BOY: 'Please believe me
    Didn't treat you fair
    But you know I care

> If you stay right here
> Gonna make it square
> I love you'

ALL: 'Yeah, yeah, yeah'

ZOMBIE BOY: 'My polar bear'

ALL: 'My polar bear
> Yeah, yeah, yeah
> My polar bear'

The cast dance slow-motion 'cosmic wormhole' moves. MOTOR-MOUTH *and* SUCK-FACE *appear downstage—speaking to each other on smartphones.*

MOTOR-MOUTH: [*spoken*] Suck-face, it's me. I know I said I would go to Blasko's party. I know, I know, but after careful strategic revision the only explanation I can give for agreeing to the loss of our respective virginities is that I was out of my freaking mind.

Pause.

Are you there?

SUCK-FACE: Motor-mouth.

MOTOR-MOUTH: Yes, Suck-face?

SUCK-FACE: In what year did Albert Einstein apply $E = MC^2$ to prove the existence of cosmic wormholes? Ten seconds, your time starts now.

MOTOR-MOUTH: Primordial or inter-dimensional cosmic wormholes?

SUCK-FACE: Primordial.

MOTOR-MOUTH: 1935.

SUCK-FACE: Correct. What scientific theory suggests the human soul is located in the stem cells of the brain?

MOTOR-MOUTH: Quantum Theory of Consciousness.

SUCK-FACE: Correct. Feeling better?

MOTOR-MOUTH: Heart rate almost normal. Blood pressure one-thirty over ninety.

SUCK-FACE: Last question, bonus points. What mammal species is currently circumnavigating the earth on the brink of extinction?

MOTOR-MOUTH: Polar bear.

SUCK-FACE: [*making a buzzer sound*] Ehhhh! Sexy Latin name please. Five seconds, four, three, two—time's up.

MOTOR-MOUTH: [*sexy voice*] Ursus maritimus.

SUCK-FACE: Congratulations, you get to go to a real party. Have real sex and smoke real dope in someone else's real bedroom.

MOTOR-MOUTH: In one night you want to make the quantum leap from kissing straight to a public exchange of reproductive bodily fluids and illegal substance abuse.

SUCK-FACE: You're hyperventilating, aren't you?

MOTOR-MOUTH: My CO_2 levels are well below critical.

SUCK-FACE: Switch on your 'what-cha-ma-call-it-brainwave-thingy'.

MOTOR-MOUTH: My Electro-Magnetic Anxiety Extractor is only for use in extreme emergencies.

SUCK-FACE: I am not going to be the only virgin left on the planet.

MOTOR-MOUTH: We can be virgins together, there's dignity in that, religious and pagan significance. Besides, extracting brainwaves is a very delicate operation.

SUCK-FACE: So is losing my virginity—which is never going to happen if you pass out and hit your head again.

MOTOR-MOUTH *reveals a formidable piece of scientific apparatus—not unlike a large salad bowl covered with wires and flashing lights.*

MOTOR-MOUTH: You do realise it's not the end of the world just because Blasko Tupper throws an end-of-the-world party.

SUCK-FACE: Did you remember the superglue and the condoms?

MOTOR-MOUTH: Yes. Did you remember to run a background check?

SUCK-FACE: I hacked into her CIA file.

MOTOR-MOUTH: She has a CIA file?

SUCK-FACE: A redacted CIA file.

MOTOR-MOUTH: Which is an alarming piece of information about someone we've only known a week.

SUCK-FACE: Switch on your 'what-cha-ma-call-it-brainwave-thingy'.

MOTOR-MOUTH: Electro-Magnetic Anxiety Extractor.

SUCK-FACE: Motor-mouth!

MOTOR-MOUTH *places his invention on his head. Lights start to blink and a fan on top whirs.*

Are you there?

MOTOR-MOUTH: I'm waiting for my CO_2 levels to adjust.

SUCK-FACE: Please don't make me explain … I just … I need you to do this with me.

MOTOR-MOUTH: Suck-face.

SUCK-FACE: Yes, Motor-mouth?

> *Beat.*

MOTOR-MOUTH: I love you.

> *Beat.*

SUCK-FACE: Motor-mouth.

MOTOR-MOUTH: Yes, Suck-face?

SUCK-FACE: Make sure you bring the superglue, your 'whatcha-ma-call-it'—and *two* condoms. I've been practising with a slinky over my bedpost—but we shouldn't take any chances.

> *The cast snap out of their 'cosmic wormhole' moves—back into the party.*

ZOMBIE BOY: [*singing*] 'Waves are crashing near Hawaii'

ALL: 'Hashtag: ten metres high'

ZOMBIE BOY: 'You're slowly sinking near the beach'

ALL: 'Going down, going down, going down'

ZOMBIE BOY: 'Your iceberg's tilting at an angle'

ALL: 'Whoa'

ZOMBIE BOY: 'Shrinking slowly out of reach'

ALL: 'Baby, baby, baby, bay-bee, bee-baby'

ZOMBIE BOY: 'Baby, swim to the shore
              Go find yourself a zoo
              Don't you know you're the only one tell me'

ALL: 'What can I do?'

ZOMBIE BOY: 'Polar bear'

ALL: 'Polar bear'

ZOMBIE BOY: 'There's only you, my polar bear'

ALL: 'Polar bear'

ZOMBIE BOY: 'Come up for air
              There is only you—know it isn't fair
              If you make it back—I will do my share
              I love you'

ALL: 'Yeah, yeah, yeah
              My polar bear'

ZOMBIE BOY: 'My polar bear'

ALL: 'Yeah, yeah, yeah
              My polar bear'

The party continues. Meanwhile ZACK *is investigating a cage covered by a satin cloth—like a magician's trick.* SARAH *tries to drag him away.*

Above the satin-covered cage is a sign with the words 'DO NOT FEED THE PARENTS' writ large.

HILARY: [*spoken*] My BuzzFeed says it's the last polar bear on the planet.

TIFFANY: Maybe we should start one of those, like—Twitter protests.

HUGO: Whoa, man—the whole freaking world is tracking this polar bear.

SARAH: Zack!

ZACK: Do not feed the parents.

SARAH: Blasko said not to touch. Her party. Her surprise.

ZACK: If not to touch why leave it here?

SARAH: Part of the fun. Armageddon, remember—prepare to die?

TIFFANY: Snapchat. Polar bear just surfed a five-metre wave off Waikiki.

HILARY: Hashtag: hang ten?

HUGO: Hashtag: wipeout.

TANK: Hashtag: we're all going to hell—da.

HUGO: [*singing*] 'Will you vanish?
　　　　Would you dare?'

SARAH:　　'You keep the faith now
　　　　Send up a flare'

TANK:　　'Can't you see?
　　　　We couldn't bear'

ALL:　　'This lonely world without you there
　　　　Yeah, yeah, yeah, yeah'

ZACK:　　'Polar bear
　　　　Won't you answer'

ALL:　　'Polar bear, polar bear?'

SARAH:　　'How can I live if you're not there
　　　　Polar bear?'

ZACK:　　'Won't you please come up for air?
　　　　I swear I love you'

ALL:　　'Yeah, yeah, yeah
　　　　My polar bear'

ZOMBIE BOY: 'My polar bear'

ALL:　　'Yeah, yeah, yeah
　　　　My polar bear'

ZOMBIE BOY: 'My polar bear'
ALL: 'Yeah, yeah, yeah
            My polar bear'

> MOTOR-MOUTH *and* SUCK-FACE *have arrived.* SUCK-FACE *is holding a balloon.*

BLASKO: [*spoken*] Welcome to my party—one-week-old friends. Such a short time to make your acquaintance, such a long time in the life of a mayfly. Eat, drink, be merry. Croquet on the lawn, dance floor on the tennis court, free nachos by the pool—but be careful. I wouldn't want anyone to drown before the apocalypse.

TIFFANY: Wow—Blasko's really getting into her end-of-the-world theme.

HUGO: Armageddon, man—radical idea for a party.

TANK: [*to* HUGO] Better than come dressed as your favourite hot dog—da.

SARAH: Hey, Blasko—Zack wants to know how we're all going to die.

HUGO: I vote killer asteroid.

ZACK: Alien invasion, man.

HILARY: World War Three?

BLASKO: Excellent ideas—but no. We all die when a solar flare strikes the earth—amplifying the effects of global warming, incinerating every creature on the face of the planet.

TIFFANY: So … does that mean there's going to be like, a fireworks display?

BLASKO: Oh, yes. But that's not important right now. What's important is stay calm, do not panic, and most important of all …

> BLASKO *rips the satin cover off the cage—revealing her parents inside, bound and gagged.*

Do not feed the parents!

> *Everyone turns to the audience.*

SARAH: [*to the audience*] So, at this point—we're all thinking the same thing.

HUGO: Best party ever!

TIFFANY: But, like, lay off the ecstasy, girl.

ZACK: Are they really her parents?

TANK: How did she get them in the cage—da?

The electric fence flashes.

BLASKO: [*To the audience*] What I haven't told them yet, is the part about the bomb. Or the part about sending their consciousness through a cosmic wormhole. Come to think of it—I also forgot to tell them the part about merging their consciousness with their other-dimensional brain. We've only known each other a week. I wouldn't want to overshare.

Crazy wormhole dancing. Time travel grooving.

SONG: 'WORMHOLE, BABY, AH HUH, AH HUH'

ZOMBIE BOY: [*singing*] 'Wormhole baby—ah huh, ah huh
            A week ago, baby—ah huh, ah huh
            Other dimensions, solar inventions
            Armageddon moves
            Quantum theory grooves
            Yeah baby, yeah baby
            Wormhole, baby—ah huh, ah huh
            A week ago, baby—ah huh, ah huh
            Time travel, baby—ah huh, ah huh
            A week ago, baby—ah huh, ah huh
            Wheeeee!'

SCENE THREE

Schoolyard. One week earlier. TIFFANY, SARAH, ZACK, MOTOR-MOUTH, SUCK-FACE, HILARY, TANK *and* HUGO *are straggled around a dead rose bush standing forlornly in a pot.*

TIFFANY: Quiet! Firstly, let me open this meeting of our 'Save The Planet Club' by thanking everyone for their *tra-mun-dous* efforts at the fundraising triathlon last weekend. Now, I know it's a bit of a bummer that our science teacher Professor Pluto had to like, 'drown' during the bathtub race—*but*—on the bright side we raised three hundred and forty-two dollars for our charity of the month …

She indicates to SARAH.

SARAH: Greenpeace.

TIFFANY: Which still left, like—

SARAH: Nine dollars—

TIFFANY: To buy this rose bush for his funeral on Friday.

HILARY: Question. Why a rose bush?

TANK: Tiffany, you have a piercing in your nose—da.

TIFFANY: It's a diamante stud encased in twenty-four-carat gold, you feral, *and* this rose bush is like something his widow can, you know, grow in her garden to remember him by.

HUGO: Yeah! No. Wait.

TANK: I'm the only one in this club who wears a nose stud.

HUGO: Tank's right, dude—you're unfairly trespassing on her carefully constructed neo-punk identity.

TANK: And you're wearing a nose stud—*da*.

SARAH: This rose bush is dead.

TIFFANY: Don't look at me—I bought the card.

SARAH: Zack?

ZACK: It's not dead—it's dying.

HUGO: Yeah! No. Wait.

ZACK: Dead would signify a callous finality. Dying implies a universal journey of rebirth.

HUGO: Is donating your brain to science tax deductible?

SUCK-FACE: It should be. Professor Pluto's brain was very special.

MOTOR-MOUTH: On the verge of inventing a revolutionary solar panel that could reduce the effects of climate change by over ten percent.

HUGO: That is so cool.

MOTOR-MOUTH: Actually it's warm.

    Pause.

    Climate change. Warm.

HILARY: I love it when you're pedantic.

SUCK-FACE: Back off, Hilary, or the next funeral will be yours.

SARAH: We're not giving his grieving widow an existential metaphor.

ZACK: It's poetry.

SARAH: It's deceased.

TIFFANY: What-*evah*. She can use it to stake tomatoes or something. Next item on the agenda. New girl arriving today.

ZACK: The girl from Germany?

HILARY: I heard she was Russian.

SUCK-FACE: Her passport says she was born in Iceland.

HILARY: Suck-face has been surfing the dark web again.

SUCK-FACE: Only for background checks. And buying fresh meat for my anaconda.

TIFFANY: Well, I heard her parents own a mansion in Brighton *and*— she's on a first-name basis with Selena Gomez.

HUGO: Wow—Selena Gomez is so into body piercing right now.

TANK: Out with the signature piece of jewellery, bitch.

TIFFANY: Eat shit and die, feral.

> TANK *attacks* TIFFANY. SUCK-FACE *and* HILARY *circle* MOTOR-MOUTH.

MOTOR-MOUTH: Traditionally of course, body piercing has its origins in central Africa, though often coincides with a distinctly rebellious phase in modern youth.

> *A bell note from the piano. The* TEENAGERS *are sucked out of the fight into cosmic wormhole slow-mo movement.*

> BLASKO *sits with her parents,* PENELOPE *and* CHRISTOPHER, *over a candlelit dinner.*

BLASKO: Mother, father, I have something I must tell you.

CHRISTOPHER: Would you pass the caviar *mon cherie*?

PENELOPE: Is that wise dear? You know how Armageddon affects your large intestine.

BLASKO: I have decided to save the planet.

CHRISTOPHER: Now Blasko, what have we told you about saving the planet?

PENELOPE: You save one planet you have to save them all.

CHRISTOPHER: Pass the wafers please.

PENELOPE: Where does it end?

CHRISTOPHER: It doesn't end. And the cheese platter.

BLASKO: But I will have my new friends to help me.

PENELOPE: Friends. What friends?

CHRISTOPHER: Now Blasko, what have we told you about friends?

PENELOPE: [*To Christopher*] Let me handle this dear.

SONG: 'REASON TO LIVE'

BLASKO: [*to the audience, singing*] 'My name is Blasko Tupper
But who I am is a mystery
My parents aren't like others
That much is clear to me
But who am I?
What is my purpose?
Is there more beneath the surface?
Should I turn it loose?'

CHRISTOPHER: [*Spoken*] You are not like other teenagers Blasko.

PENELOPE: This family is not like other families.

BLASKO: I know but—
[*Singing*] 'I have to try, which is why
I've drugged your salmon mousse

PENELOPE *and* CHRISTOPHER*'s heads splat into their dinner plates.*

I have stolen secrets
From the sultan of Brunei
Learned to cheat a lie detector
Fake an alibi

I've planted drugs on presidents
In Russia and Dubai
But have never thought
To ask the question why
What's the point in always taking
Never to give
Without sharing, without caring
Is there a reason to live?
And if I exist—and I exist—must I be an island?
Alone with nothing to give
Without a reason to live'

The cast are sucked back into their normal world. TIFFANY *places a ribbon on the dead rose bush.*

TIFFANY: [*spoken*] *Ta–da!*

HILARY: Question. If they're burying Professor Pluto's body—but donating his brain to science—shouldn't we be buying *two* dead rose bushes?

SARAH: The best teacher in the whole school.

TANK: The guy was a freaking genius.

TIFFANY: He gave me an A for making organic mascara.

SUCK-FACE: If only he'd finished his solar panel *before* he pulled the plug out of his bathtub.

ZACK: You think they'll store his brain in a museum?

TANK: Probably some sick laboratory.

HILARY: Floating in a jar—strapped with electrodes—waiting to be dissected.

HUGO: [*singing*] 'If your body's buried
          And your brain is in a jar'

MOTOR-MOUTH
& SUCK-FACE: 'Could you still be conscious
          And aware of who you are?'

SARAH: 'Is your soul in heaven'

TANK: 'And connected from afar'

HUGO, HILARY
& TIFFANY: 'Or is it stuck forever
          With your brain inside the jar?'

ALL: 'Do we go on
          Needing answers no-one can give?
          Are we ever free from uncertainty?
          Is there a reason to live?
          If I exist—and I exist—there must be a purpose
          An answer someone can give
          Somewhere a reason to live
          Aye ka-rum-ba!'

TIFFANY: [*spoken*] So, Blasko. What kind of name *is* Blasko—German, Dutch?

BLASKO: Icelandic.

HUGO: Yo—cool.

BLASKO: Yes, very.

SARAH: We heard you were in Brazil before you came here.

BLASKO: Actually, I was in a small village on the Amazon River while my parents completed their advanced diploma in voodoo mind control.

TIFFANY: Is that where you met Selena Gomez? I hear she's like, totally into voodoo mind control.

BLASKO: [*speaking into her watch*] Monday morning, oh-eight hundred hours. Psychological analysis of student two-three-two indicates extreme insecurity, low self-esteem. Estimated chance of survival—twenty percent.

SUCK-FACE: She's talking into her watch, Motor-mouth.

MOTOR-MOUTH: You talk into your watch.

SUCK-FACE: Only when I'm pretending to be Captain Kirk.

SARAH: You know, Blasko, I have the strangest feeling we've met before.

BLASKO: Your name is Sarah.

SARAH: That's right.

BLASKO: And the two of us made passionate love on top of the Eiffel Tower last Bastille Day.

SARAH: No! That's not me. I didn't—

BLASKO: Interesting. [*Into her watch*] Analysis of student two-five-one indicates elevated levels of homosexual paranoia requiring further investigation.

HILARY: Question. If you've never met—how did you know her name?

BLASKO: I have memorised the names, telephone numbers and postcodes of all two hundred and fifty-three students at this school. Isn't that right, Zack, boyfriend of Sarah?

ZACK: You are weird.

BLASKO: And you are a very strong man with a long reach from palm to armpit. That's going to come in handy if you ever have to wield a machete.

SARAH: How did you get the names of every student at the school?

BLASKO: I hacked into your Department of Education.

HUGO: Whoa, man, isn't that illegal?

BLASKO: Not in North Korea. You! Tank Ramone. How much can you bench press?

TANK: Da?

BLASKO: These are well-defined biceps. Either you have access to a former Eastern Bloc gymnastics coach or you work out. How much?

TANK: Sixty-five kilos.

BLASKO: Impressive. Although I once met a girl who could bench press a hundred and sixty-five kilos. But she had access to a former Eastern Bloc gymnastics coach.

SARAH: What did you say your parents did for a living?

BLASKO: I didn't.

TIFFANY: Right. But, like, they must work for someone.

BLASKO: My parents work for anyone who can afford them.

HUGO: Whoa, man—how rich are you?

BLASKO: [*deadly serious*] Money isn't important.

A quick succession of secret-dark-art-spy moves—then pause.

Information is important.

Beat.

HUGO: [*lost for words*] Right.

TIFFANY: Wow.

TANK: Da.

Pregnant pause as BLASKO *holds her dark-art-spy move pose.*

SARAH: Soooo.

TIFFANY: Like.

HUGO: Wow. Information.

Beat.

You mean like Foxtel?

BLASKO: [*into the watch*] Research log. Update student two-two-nine. Subject highly intelligent, feigns stupidity. Analysis indicates use of recreational drugs and promiscuous sexual activity.

HUGO: That is, like, freaky accurate.

HILARY: Question. If you're rich why are you going to school here?

BLASKO: I heard about your science teacher—and his revolutionary solar panel.

SUCK-FACE: Professor Pluto died in a terrible accident.

BLASKO: Yes. And no. But that's not important right now. What's important is this. Professor Pluto was a free thinker. I am a free thinker. [*Pointing, emphatic*] Are you free thinkers?

HILARY: I hide video cameras in the boy's toilet.

SUCK-FACE: I hack into the KGB to steal information about Lady Gaga.

MOTOR-MOUTH: I invent computer applications and associated devices.

BLASKO: Explosive devices?

TIFFANY: You did that one time.

MOTOR-MOUTH: My Bunsen burner malfunctioned.
BLASKO: Congratulations!
    [*Singing*] 'You're not exactly "a" team
    Or "b"—or even "c"—or "d"
    But you want to save the world
    And that is good enough for me
    Come get your invitation
    Here, before they disappear

BLASKO *hands out invitations.*

    Don't miss out
    It's sure to be the party of the year'
TIFFANY: 'We're going to a party'
BLASKO: 'Let down your hair
    The end of the world
    See you all there'
TANK: 'End of the world—da?'
TIFFANY: 'What should we wear?'
BLASKO: 'A little black dress—oh! And clean underwear
    What's the point in always lying never to live?
    Why be hiding, not confiding
    If you have something to give?'
ALL: 'For if I exist—and I exist
    There must be a reason
    An answer someone can give'
BLASKO: [*spoken*] It's party time!
ALL: 'A reason to
    Reason to live'

Music. ZOMBIE *rampage.* ZOMBIE BOY *in the middle of the chaos.*

SONG: 'WORMHOLE, BABY'—REPRISE

ZOMBIE BOY: [*singing*] 'Wormhole, baby—ah huh, ah huh
    A week from now, baby—ah huh, ah huh
    Time travel, baby—ah huh, ah huh
    A week from now, baby—ah huh, ah huh
    Wheeeeeee!'

The cast collapse on the ground—dead ZOMBIES.

SCENE FOUR

A week later. The end of the party. PENELOPE *and* CHRISTOPHER TUPPER *emerge from their cage and greet a police officer who is invisible to the audience. They are dressed in elegant, expensive clothing.* CHRISTOPHER*'s hand is bandaged.*

PENELOPE: Good morning, officer. My name is Penelope Tupper and this is my husband.

CHRISTOPHER: Christopher Tupper.

PENELOPE: He can't shake your hand.

SONG: 'HAND OVER THE GUN'

CHRISTOPHER: [*singing*] 'I have a burn'
PENELOPE: 'A nasty burn'
CHRISTOPHER: 'A nasty burn from the explosion'
PENELOPE: 'The explosion, officer'
CHRISTOPHER: 'Nasty burn'
PENELOPE: 'We'd like to thank you
              For the way you cleared the bomb'
CHRISTOPHER: 'You cleared zee bomb'
PENELOPE: 'Put out the fire'
CHRISTOPHER: 'Nasty fire'
PENELOPE: 'Bagged the bodies'
CHRISTOPHER: 'Nasty bodies'
PENELOPE: 'As you see, the party went off with a bang'
CHRISTOPHER: 'Forgive zee pun'

> *They attempt to hypnotise the police officer using voodoo mind control. The* TEENAGERS *come back to life—at the party.* SUCK-FACE *is holding a balloon. Two different moments in time.*

BOTH: 'Now hand over the gun'
CHRISTOPHER: 'You will—'
PENELOPE: 'Look into my eyes'
BOTH: 'You will hand over the—'
PENELOPE: I beg your pardon, officer?
CHRISTOPHER: [*singing*] 'Bodies!'

PENELOPE: 'Yes, the bodies'
CHRISTOPHER: 'Lots of bodies'
PENELOPE: 'By the pool'
CHRISTOPHER: 'You should investigate'
PENELOPE: 'Our daughter'
CHRISTOPHER: 'Yes, our daughter'
PENELOPE: 'Should investigate'
CHRISTOPHER: 'A tragedy'
PENELOPE: 'We have no explanation'
CHRISTOPHER: 'For her actions'
PENELOPE: 'Yes, high-spirited'
CHRISTOPHER: 'Intelligent'
PENELOPE: 'Well-travelled'
CHRISTOPHER: 'Yes, we travel'
PENELOPE: 'We're consultants'
CHRISTOPHER: 'We consult'
PENELOPE: 'On different issues'
CHRISTOPHER: 'Global warming'
PENELOPE: 'Corporate tax evasion'
CHRISTOPHER: 'Fake news'
PENELOPE: 'Elections'
CHRISTOPHER: 'We create'
PENELOPE: 'The right perception'
CHRISTOPHER: 'We are'
PENELOPE: 'Information specialists'
CHRISTOPHER: 'For corporations'
PENELOPE: 'ASIO'
CHRISTOPHER: 'The CIA—whoever can afford us'
PENELOPE: 'Manufacturing'
CHRISTOPHER: 'The truth'
PENELOPE: 'Is that we spin'
CHRISTOPHER: 'We spin'
PENELOPE: 'We spin'
CHRISTOPHER: 'Whatever's spinning'
PENELOPE: 'We'll have spun'
BOTH: 'Now hand over the gun'
CHRISTOPHER: 'You will—'

PENELOPE: 'Look into my eyes'
CHRISTOPHER: 'You will—'
PENELOPE: 'Look into my—'
BOTH: 'You will hand over the gun
            Will hand over the—'

    MOTOR-MOUTH *dances the macarena around* CHRISTOPHER *and*
    PENELOPE, *wearing the Electro-Magnetic Anxiety Extractor on*
    his head.

PENELOPE: I'm sorry, officer? You were saying—
CHRISTOPHER: Who is this young man with the strange apparatus on
  his head?
PENELOPE: Oh—just some delirious boy from the party.
CHRISTOPHER: You know how teenagers can be.
PENELOPE: Rebellious.
CHRISTOPHER: Irresponsible.
PENELOPE: He could be dangerous.
CHRISTOPHER: Completely deranged.
PENELOPE: You should take out your weapon.
CHRISTOPHER: While there's still time.
PENELOPE: [*singing*] 'Wait! is that the time?'
CHRISTOPHER: 'The time?'
PENELOPE: 'Yes—Eastern Standard Time'
CHRISTOPHER: 'My watch is gone'
PENELOPE: 'Our daughter stole them'
CHRISTOPHER: 'Officer?'
PENELOPE: 'You said the time was—'
CHRISTOPHER: 'That's the time?'
PENELOPE: 'Oh dear, it's late'
CHRISTOPHER: 'It's very late'
PENELOPE: 'We should be going'
CHRISTOPHER: 'Very late!'
PENELOPE: 'We shouldn't keep you from the—'
CHRISTOPHER: 'Bodies!'
PENELOPE: 'Lots of—'
CHRISTOPHER: 'Bodies!'
PENELOPE: 'Well, goodbye, been so much fun'

CHRISTOPHER: 'Before we go'
PENELOPE: 'We have to run'
CHRISTOPHER: 'Give us the gun'
PENELOPE: 'Been so much fun'
CHRISTOPHER: 'Before we're done'
PENELOPE: 'The freaking gun!'
BOTH: 'You must hand over the gun'
CHRISTOPHER: 'You will—'
PENELOPE: 'Look into my eyes'
CHRISTOPHER: 'You will—'
PENELOPE: 'Look into my eyes'
CHRISTOPHER: 'You will'
TEENAGERS: 'Five'
BOTH: 'Hand over the—'
TEENAGERS: 'Four'
BOTH: 'Hand over the—'
TEENAGERS: 'Three'
BOTH: 'Hand over the—'
TEENAGERS: 'Two, one'
BOTH: 'Gun!'

SCENE FIVE

Schoolyard. Three days before the party.

SONG: 'WANNA EAT YOUR BRAIN'

ZOMBIE BOY: [*singing*] 'Baby, this is my dimension
            Baby, that is your dimension
            Don't wanna cramp your style or cause you pain
            So what if some cosmic wormhole
            Can merge my soul with your soul?
            Baby, I just wanna eat your brain

            Don't wanna look for answers
            Don't wanna have to feel
            Just want to drink your plasma
            With a slice of lemon peel
            Don't want to solve no mysteries

Don't want to take a stance
I just want your cranium for
Sweet and hot romance

SARAH *is practising martial arts on* ZACK. MOTOR-MOUTH *is nearby, eating a sandwich.*

Baby, this is my dimension—
Baby, that is your dimension
Don't wanna cramp your style or cause you pain
So what if some cosmic wormhole
Can merge my soul with your soul?
To be that close would be insane
There's no getting off that train
Baby, I just want to eat your brain'

SARAH: [*spoken*] Blasko's party this Saturday. I heard she's invited over a hundred kids.

ZACK: [*to the audience*] Sarah likes parties. Sarah likes to kiss in a corner pretending the wind is cold.

SARAH: You think it's wrong celebrating the day after Professor Pluto's funeral? I heard the Russians bought his brain for like, a million dollars.

ZACK: They say the last polar bear on the planet will die Saturday night.

SARAH: I heard that too.

ZACK: Think of it like another funeral. Together, shall we weep, beneath the melancholy constellations. [*To audience*] Sarah loves poetry.

SARAH *throws* ZACK *to the ground and sits on him.*

SARAH: Do you ever feel like we knew each other before we were us? Reincarnation, that's what this feels like.

ZACK: Yet all I feel is shame and filth.

SARAH: The world would be so freaking lonely without you.

ZACK: [*to the audience*] When I'm alone with her I can barely breathe.

SARAH: You make me feel so safe.

ZACK: [*to* SARAH] I can't breathe.

SARAH *lets him up. They sit together.*

SARAH: It's getting cold. Should have brought a coat.

ZACK: [*singing*] 'Cold as Judas piss oe'r the sea
Where white gulls shit their black remorse'

SARAH: [*spoken*] Good thing I have you to keep me warm.
ZOMBIE BOY: [*singing*] 'Wanna eat your brain
              Wanna eat your brain'
SARAH: 'We live to be loved
              The crown of our existence
              An ocean of forever
              Where the galleon of immortality floats
              When you look into my eyes
              And recognise the truth of my soul'
ZACK: 'The most popular girl in the school'
SARAH: 'Beyond the wind, beyond the stars'
ZACK: 'Her mouth so needing me to ache
              Yet all I feel'
SARAH: 'My ever-ness and never-ness'
ZACK: 'Plunge the knife, you freaking coward'
SARAH: [*spoken*] I love you, Zack.
ZACK: I know.

SCENE SIX

Schoolyard. Lights cross to MOTOR-MOUTH *eating a sandwich. Pretending not to watch him—and eating her own sandwich—is* HILARY.

HILARY: Tuna?
MOTOR-MOUTH: Fishpaste.
HILARY: Protein.
MOTOR-MOUTH: Vitamins A, D and C, which protect the immune system against unforeseen pandemics such as bird flu, smallpox or the Ebola virus.
HILARY: [*her sandwich*] Cheese and Vegemite.
MOTOR-MOUTH: Calcium and Vitamin B.
HILARY: I love the way you take care of your body, Motor-mouth. Do you ever stand in front of the mirror naked—fantasising your rippling muscles clutching a rocket-launcher in the ravished wastelands of World War Three?

    Pause.

MOTOR-MOUTH: Yes. But only when I overindulge on Wizz Fizz.

HILARY: Suck-face is incapable of passion.

MOTOR-MOUTH: Hilary, I don't want hurt your feelings. I just want to be friends.

> *Pause.*

HILARY: Friends.

MOTOR-MOUTH: Yes.

HILARY: Really.

MOTOR-MOUTH: Yes.

HILARY: That's not what you say in your letter. You remember. [*Holding a letter*] The letter you sent me in Grade Four.

MOTOR-MOUTH: We were ten years old.

HILARY: You wrote like you were thirty-five and Spanish.

SONG: 'SU PASTA DE PESCADO'

HILARY: [*singing as she reads*] 'I long to taste my fishpaste
   On your fingertips
   Quiero probar
   Su pasta de pescado on my lips'

MOTOR-MOUTH: [*spoken*] I never should have used Google Translator.

HILARY: 'Let me taste your tuna on my tongue
   Like before when we were young
   What does she have that I don't?
   What will she do that I won't?
   Let us eat lunch
   Let me munch on your face—Romeo
   Quiero probar su pasta de pescado

> HILARY *dances the macarena—wooing* MOTOR-MOUTH—*as he tries to retrieve the letter.*

   I long to share my vitamin B one and two
   Tengo que morder la
   Ve-he-mite sandwich with you
   I know you feel the heat
   Hear the heart inside me beat
   She makes you a mouse, not a man
   Can she say "I love you"? I can
   I won't retreat

> I'm your fishpaste to eat—let her go
> Quiero probar su pasta de pescado'

MOTOR-MOUTH *snatches the letter from* HILARY *just as* SUCK-FACE *enters with her anaconda in a carry bag—the bag is jerking, wildly.*

SUCK-FACE: [*spoken*] Motor-mouth?

MOTOR-MOUTH: Suck-face!

SUCK-FACE: You're supposed to be completing your risk assessment for Blasko's party.

MOTOR-MOUTH: I am. Yes. Just as soon as I recalibrate my Electro-Magnetic Anxiety Extractor.

SUCK-FACE: Have you been testing that 'brainwave thingy' on my anaconda?

MOTOR-MOUTH: Not exactly. That is, I may have, you know, accidentally reversed the polarity, thereby transferring some of my brainwaves into your 'eunectes murinus'. But I'm sure it won't produce any long-term psychological damage.

SUCK-FACE: He's developed a stutter, Motor-mouth. And if I didn't know better I'd say he was dancing the macarena.

HILARY: I'm angry and ugly. No-one ever saw through that but you.

SUCK-FACE: Why does the macarena make your brainwaves anxious?

MOTOR-MOUTH: I have a bad feeling about this party. Wouldn't you prefer a romantic dinner for two?

HILARY: She cares more about that snake than you.

MOTOR-MOUTH: Actually, the anaconda is technically a python.

HILARY: [*singing*] 'Her soul burns no fire
> No love or desire
> Her heart strings aren't plucked
> She's a vixen, a bimbo
> She'll leave you in limbo'

MOTOR-MOUTH: [*spoken*] My fishpaste is fucked.

HILARY: 'Quiero probar su pasta de pescado
> You're the salmon in my stream
> The taste of the paste in my dreams
> You're meek and mild it
> Drives me wild with fantasies

I can say "I love you"
All Suck-face does is tease
I'm the one who'll please
She'll break your heart before you know
She's not worthy of your fishpaste'

MOTOR-MOUTH: [*spoken*] I'm sorry, Hilary. I just don't love you
anymore.

He lays the letter at HILARY*'s feet. Suck-face's anaconda bag is
still jerking.* SUCK-FACE *exits and* MOTOR-MOUTH *follows.*

HILARY: [*singing*] 'Quiero probar su pasta de pescado'
ALL: 'Worm hole baby, time travel baby'

SCENE SEVEN

The party. CHRISTOPHER *and* PENELOPE *are in the cage—exposed.*
ZOMBIE BOY *picks up the letter and reads. His body responds to the
music with a Spanish-zombie-groove.*

SONG: 'WELCOME TO MY PARTY'

BLASKO: [*singing*] 'Welcome to my party
              The part-ay—to end all parties
              Did I mention the solar flare?'
ALL: 'Yeah!'
BLASKO: 'And do not feed the parents over there'
ALL: 'Do not feed the parents'
BLASKO: 'Now there's just a few more details
              Then we're on our way
              The part-ay to end all parties'

HUGO: [*spoken*] Hey, Tank, they're serving nachos by the pool.
TIFFANY: I like nachos.
HUGO: Stop staring at me.
TIFFANY: I wasn't staring. I was like, looking at the tree and your head
    got in the way.
HUGO: I know what you're thinking.
TIFFANY: I'm not thinking anything. I mean I am thinking something,
    I'm not, like, without the power of thought.
HILARY: Has anyone seen Motor-mouth and Suck-face?

TANK: Cool your engines, Hilary, they're all talk.

TIFFANY: At least somebody's getting some action.

TANK: Trust me, no-one is having sex.

HUGO: Unless it really is the end of the world, then everyone will be doing it.

TANK: Give me a good book or David Bowie any day.

Beat.

HUGO: Bowie is pretty cool.

TIFFANY: Yeah, right, I mean like—so cool.

ZACK: Apocalypse hypothetical. The last song you would ever listen to.

HUGO: 'Shine on you Crazy Diamond'—Pink Floyd.

HILARY: 'I Wanna Hold Your Hand'—Beatles.

TANK: Kylie Minogue—'Fever'.

TIFFANY: And people think I'm shallow.

TANK: Kylie beat cancer. She even managed to make short hair look good.

ZACK: How much would it suck to beat cancer, only to have the world end, like, the very next day?

HILARY: Unless the cancer was terminal—then it would be a relief.

HUGO: Or what if you knew you had cancer, right—*then* found out the world was going to end. Would you still have the treatment?

TIFFANY: What's the point? You're going to die anyway.

TANK: I have cancer. I'd have the treatment.

TIFFANY: What-evah. [*To* TANK] Wait—what did you say?

HUGO: Who cares if everything on the planet ceases to exist.

TANK: Radio waves won't cease to exist.

HUGO: Judgment day Tank, you think Triple R is gonna get an exemption?

TANK: Radio waves travel through space—da. Traveling to the farthest reaches of the universe.

HUGO: Whoa, so even if the earth was blow-torched tonight.

TANK: Somewhere in the cosmos, right this second, Elvis is singing 'Hound Dog'.

SCENE EIGHT

BLASKO *uses props to demonstrate her theory.* SUCK-FACE *is holding a balloon.*

BLASKO: [*singing*] 'Doesn't matter who you are
　　　　　　　Or where you're from
　　　　　　　To propel your consciousness you need a bomb
　　　　　　　After the bomb has gone ka-boom
　　　　　　　Your body is gone
　　　　　　　But your consciousness goes zoom
　　　　　　　Out into the cosmos
　　　　　　　Your thoughts and memories spin
　　　　　　　The cosmic wormhole's gravity is strong
　　　　　　　It sucks them in
　　　　　　　They travel through the wormhole
　　　　　　　Till a quantum intervention
　　　　　　　Spits them out into a whole other dimension
　　　　　　　Welcome to my party'
ALL: 'Gonna boom?'
BLASKO: 'The part-ay—to end all parties'
ALL: 'Gonna zoom?'
BLASKO: 'In the next dimension there's a whole other you
　　　　　　　Your consciousness is very smart
　　　　　　　It knows just what to do
　　　　　　　It merges with your other brain
　　　　　　　The knowledge starts to flow
　　　　　　　Your other brain now knows things
　　　　　　　That before it didn't know'
SARAH: [*spoken*] What do you mean bomb?
BLASKO: I mean a violent eruption of combustible chemicals causing instantaneous death just before the end of the world.
ZACK: Why would we want to blow ourselves up before Armageddon?
BLASKO: To propel our consciousness through the cosmic wormhole that will open just before the solar flare strikes—
ZACK: To send our consciousness through a cosmic wormhole that leads to a whole other—
SARAH: Dimension. And in this other dimension—
TANK: Our consciousness will like, merge with our other dimensional brains.
TIFFANY: Hello! You don't line up for the Myer stocktake sale then go buy K-Mart just before the doors open.

SUCK-FACE: [*holding a balloon*] What happens when the wormhole closes?

BLASKO: The solar flare strikes the earth and—

She pops Suck-face's balloon.

Any more questions?

HILARY: Um.

HUGO: Well.

ZACK: Yeah.

MOTOR-MOUTH: How do we blow ourselves up?

BLASKO: Beside my pool there is a giant beachball. Inside the giant beachball is twenty kilos of plastic explosive.

HUGO: Wouldn't it be easier to swallow a pill?

BLASKO: According to my parents, death must be *instantaneous!*

HUGO: What about guns?

BLASKO: Are you trained in the use of firearms?

HUGO: I play 'Call of Duty'.

BLASKO: No poison, strangulation, drowning, electrocution or accidental asphyxiation while choking on your own vomit.

SARAH: Right. So the world is going to end because your parents told you.

HILARY: Are they going to blow themselves up?

BLASKO: They are trained in the use of firearms—but I cannot permit them to travel through the wormhole. My parents are not like other parents.

Discussion. Confusion. Doubt.

SARAH: I'll do it!

ALL: [*improvised reactions*] What? / Are you nuts? / You can't be serious! / [Et cetera]

BLASKO: You will come with me into the other dimension?

SARAH: Sure, why not.

　　[*Singing*] 'I just need to see some proof
　　Before I go
　　Where's this beachball bomb
　　You're gonna blow?'

ALL: [*spoken improvised agreement*] Yeah! / Too right! / Prove it! / [Et cetera]

BLASKO:　　'I agree you need substantiation

>   So here's a smaller bomb
>   I made for demonstration

BLASKO *detonates a bomb—the party shakes, everyone screams.*

>   Welcome to my party'
ALL: 'Gonna die'
BLASKO: 'The party to end all parties'
ALL: 'Say goodbye!'
SARAH: 'If it's true we would have heard'
ZACK: 'Her whole concept is absurd'
BOTH: 'The world is not about to end, okay it's not'
ALL: 'The part-ay to end all parties'
BLASKO: [*spoken*] Do not waste your time contacting the authorities. I am jamming all telecommunications until after Armageddon.
SUCK-FACE: She's right. I have no internet.
TIFFANY: No Instagram. No Selena. I am out of here.
BLASKO: [*singing*] 'Do not try to escape
>   Do not feed the parents
>   You must decide if I am right or I am errant'
SARAH: [*spoken*] What do you mean … escape?
BLASKO: This morning I had an electric fence installed around the perimeter of this property. It comes with its own generator.

A flash of light. A scream as someone tries to escape. Lights go out.

They hold up their smartphones that no longer work. Little glowing ghosts swaying in the dark. MOTOR-MOUTH *and* SUCK-FACE *sneak away.*

>   [*Singing*] 'Look now—see—aurora australis
>   The solar flare is coming and it won't miss
>   At exactly midnight light will fill the sky
>   The wormhole will appear
>   The polar bear will die
>   Unless we are obliterated
>   Our end is also nigh
>   A living hell too horrible to mention
>   For only consciousness can pass
>   Into the next dimension'

SCENE NINE

MOTOR-MOUTH *and* SUCK-FACE *have failed in their attempt to lose their virginity.*

MOTOR-MOUTH: This is very embarrassing.
SUCK-FACE: Don't speak, Motor-mouth.
MOTOR-MOUTH: Suck-face—
SUCK-FACE: You promised your hormone levels were extremely high.
MOTOR-MOUTH: They are.
SUCK-FACE: High enough to sustain an erection for weeks on end—requiring a clinical application of cold showers, ice cubes and constant therapeutic masturbation.
MOTOR-MOUTH: It's not you, it's me. The pressure of knowing the world is about to end. A beachball filled with high explosive. I want us to remember this night for more than just one big bang.

SUCK-FACE *would be very happy with a big bang.*

SUCK-FACE: Do you remember the first time we met?
MOTOR-MOUTH: Sports carnival. We both had letters excusing us.
SUCK-FACE: You wore a pair of bicycle shorts three sizes too small.
MOTOR-MOUTH: You wore mohair bobby socks in forty-degree heat.
SUCK-FACE: You said I was beautiful—was that true?
MOTOR-MOUTH: Yes. No-one stirs my heart like you. All I require are three little words.
SUCK-FACE: All I need are two.

SONG: 'DO ME, DO ME, DO ME, DO'

> [*Singing*] 'Do me, do me, do me, do
> I surrender this body to you
> Take me and do what you will
> Take what you want and don't stop
> Until you've had your fill
> Make it wild, make it gritty
> Just make me feel pretty
> If you love me then show me it's true
> Do me, do me, do—
> Do me, do me, do me, do

Want me, want me, want me, now
Tie me up, tie me down—and then pow!
Wow me like no-one else has
Don't need Cupid and strings
When my bongos are craving your jazz
Do me hot, do me steamy
Do me slow-mo—and dreamy
Do me covered in chocolatey goo
Just do me, do me, do me
Do me, do me, do me, do'
MOTOR-MOUTH: 'You know that is not my routine
I can't turn it on, turn it off
Like some kind of machine

You want an erection
Try love and affection
The magical key to my chastity
Are three little words'
SUCK-FACE: 'Do me, do me, do me
Do me, do me, do me, do'
MOTOR-MOUTH: 'My G-spot is three, please make it three'
SUCK-FACE: 'Show me, show me, show me
Show me, show me, show me, show'
MOTOR-MOUTH: 'No, no, no, just use the key, set me free'
SUCK-FACE: 'Stop talking, start walking
My shy Stephen Hawking
Come thrill me and fill me with you
Oh God—do me, do me, do
Do me, do me, do me, do'
MOTOR-MOUTH: 'I can't, I just can't, I can't, I can't, I can't—do'
SUCK-FACE: 'If you can't then we're through'
MOTOR-MOUTH: 'We are through?'
SUCK-FACE: 'We are through'
MOTOR-MOUTH: 'Then we're through'
SUCK-FACE: 'Okay we're through'
MOTOR-MOUTH: 'We are through'
SUCK-FACE: 'We are through'
BOTH: 'We are through, we are through'

MOTOR-MOUTH *exits.*

SUCK-FACE: [*spoken*] I knew I should have worn the miniskirt.

SCENE TEN

SARAH *tries to calm an hysterical party.* HILARY *stalks the stage searching for* MOTOR-MOUTH *while* TIFFANY *is drinking heavily.*

TIFFANY: [*singing*] 'Baby, baby, we're gonna die
            Baby we're gonna fry'
SARAH: [*spoken*] We have to stay calm. The world is not going to end.
    I repeat do not panic, stay clear of the bomb.
TIFFANY: [*singing*] 'Gonna get blown sky high
            Baby, baby, baby, we're gonna die'

    TIFFANY *continues to improvise through the following dialogue.*

    ZACK *enters.*

ZACK: [*spoken*] I can't find the generator. She must have buried it
    underground.
SARAH: Get Hugo and Tank—find a shovel.
HILARY: Motor-mouth!
ZACK: I checked the shed—there's like, one blowtorch, a lawnmower
    and seven chainsaws.
TIFFANY: [*singing*] 'Die, die, die, die, die!' [Et cetera]
ZACK: Why the hell do they need seven chainsaws?
SARAH: Use one to cut through the fence.
ZACK: Ten thousand volts.
TIFFANY: Yeah—and electrocution doesn't work, remember?
HILARY: I can smell your pimple cream!
ZACK: All we have to do is wait for the cops.
SARAH: What about the bomb?
ZACK: Stay away from the pool.
SARAH: A hundred drunk, hysterical teenagers.
ZACK: No-one is going to blow themselves up.
TIFFANY: [*singing*] 'Die, die, die, die, die! Diiiiiie!'
ZACK: [*spoken*] Hugo!
HILARY: I'll find you if I have to rip this place apart one bedroom at a time.
SARAH: Didn't anyone ever tell you the fastest way to get a boy is to
    ignore them?

TIFFANY: I thought the fastest way was get drunk and put out.

HILARY: Back off, Sarah. I don't care if you have a black belt in hakki-hakki-ho. She stole him from me.

TIFFANY: You're sharing this information on the last night of the world?

SARAH: I thought you knew.

TIFFANY: I've never had a boyfriend in my life. Call yourself a friend.

SARAH: There's still an hour till the end of the world and plenty of boys to go around.

Spark and sizzle from the electric fence.

TIFFANY: Not if they keep getting electrocuted.

HILARY: Motor-mouth!

BLASKO *enters as* HILARY *exits.*

BLASKO: One hour, six minutes and eighteen seconds.

TIFFANY: I'm going to ignore boys and see if it works.

BLASKO: If it doesn't you can always drug them. I have the pills.

SARAH: Turn off the fence and let us go.

BLASKO: Face the truth. The world will end. Zack wants to break up. You are a very deluded individual.

SARAH: You're a psychopath.

BLASKO: No. A psychopath would cut off your head and paint your toe-nails black. I am trying to be your friend.

SARAH: Friends don't manipulate each other.

MOTOR-MOUTH *enters upstage, drunk on Wizz Fizz.*

MOTOR-MOUTH: Friends don't place unreasonable ultimatums on their relationship.

SARAH: Getting us pissed, ramping up the paranoia.

MOTOR-MOUTH: Friends display a mutual understanding of each other's emotional complexity.

SARAH: You're screwing with our heads.

BLASKO: No. That would be extremely messy, not to mention unhygienic.

MOTOR-MOUTH: I believe Sarah is referring to the way you employ misdirection to avoid addressing an otherwise straightforward question.

BLASKO: Sarah hasn't asked a question, she just keeps making statements.

MOTOR-MOUTH: You did it again.

BLASKO: I did?

SARAH: Yes!

BLASKO: My parents do it all the time. But I am telling you the truth.

SARAH: You didn't pick our school by accident. You knew our names, you knew everything about us.

MOTOR-MOUTH: Perhaps now would be a good time to tell her about Professor Pluto's brain.

SARAH: Excuse me?

BLASKO: What do you know about Professor Pluto's brain?

MOTOR-MOUTH: I know you keep it in a pickle jar.

BLASKO: How do you know that?

MOTOR-MOUTH: You don't know how I know? I assume the same way your parents know about Armageddon [*hic*] quantum consciousness, the cosmic wormhole [*hic*].

SARAH: Have you been drinking?

MOTOR-MOUTH: Negative. I overdosed on Wizz Fizz. But that's not important right now. What's important is this …

> TANK *and* HUGO *appear in an echo of their earlier scene.* BLASKO *retrieves Professor Pluto's brain from its hiding place.*

TANK: Radio waves …

MOTOR-MOUTH: Radio waves and satellite signals travel through space and time.

TANK: Travelling to the farthest reaches of the galaxy.

BLASKO: [*with the brain*] Carrying information from one dimension to another.

MOTOR-MOUTH: Not just one dimension. Billions of dimensions.

BLASKO: Dimensions where the world is already over.

MOTOR-MOUTH: Dimensions where this party is yet to happen.

HUGO: Whoa, so even if the earth was blowtorched tonight.

TANK: Somewhere in the cosmos, right this second, Elvis is singing 'Hound Dog'.

BLASKO: And Professor Pluto is still alive.

> BLASKO *hands Professor Pluto's brain—inside a pickle jar—to* SARAH.

SARAH: You have got to be shitting me.

BLASKO: I left a lovely card next to your dead rose bush.

SARAH: *You* stole his brain?

BLASKO: No. I paid a million dollars for it using my parents' black Visa card. it's a very special brain.

MOTOR-MOUTH: On the verge of inventing a revolutionary solar panel.

BLASKO: A solar panel that could save the next dimension.

SARAH: How?

BLASKO: By absorbing enough radiation to prevent the solar flare from amplifying the effects of global warming.

MOTOR-MOUTH: You see, in theory, this brain's consciousness already contains the knowledge he needs to complete his invention.

BLASKO: So technically speaking, if we wait for the wormhole to open then blow up 'this' brain—

MOTOR-MOUTH: The 'knowledge' in this brain will be transferred to his 'other- dimensional' brain.

BLASKO: So he can finish his solar panel and save the planet—

MOTOR-MOUTH: Before he dies in a bathtub race.

> *Beat.*

ALL: [*together*] In the other dimension.

SARAH: Does a brain in a pickle jar have a consciousness?

BLASKO: Oh, yes. And no.

MOTOR-MOUTH: Without a body his brainwaves have probably gone into hibernation.

BLASKO: Which means the odds of success are approximately … a million to one.

SARAH: A million to one?

BLASKO: That's the bad news.

MOTOR-MOUTH: What's the good news?

BLASKO: There's a first time for everything. Fifty-nine minutes, twenty-two seconds and counting.

SONG: 'TO GET THE JOB DONE'

ZOMBIE BOY: [*singing*] 'You want to save the other dimension?
          Gonna need a solar invention
          That flare is gonna burn so hot
          You're only gonna get one shot
          But two brains are better than one
          It takes two brains, baby, to get the job done'

SCENE ELEVEN

HILARY *is crying.* CHRISTOPHER *and* PENELOPE *watch from the cage—they have managed to free their hands and remove their gags.*

CHRISTOPHER: [*to* HILARY] Hello, little girl, little girl, over here.
PENELOPE: Pretty little girl, isn't she? Positively divine.
CHRISTOPHER: What is your name, little girl?
HILARY: Hilary.
CHRISTOPHER & PENELOPE: [*together*] Hilary!
PENELOPE: Extraordinary.
CHRISTOPHER: The name of a Russian princess.
HILARY: What princess?
PENELOPE: Why, princess Hilary of Russia, of course.
CHRISTOPHER: Have you seen our daughter? Your Royal Highness.
PENELOPE: She's been a very naughty girl.
HILARY: She drugged your salmon mousse.
PENELOPE: Yes, she did.
CHRISTOPHER: That was very clever of her.
PENELOPE: Yes it was, very—
CHRISTOPHER: Very—
CHRISTOPHER & PENELOPE: [*together*] Clever.
CHRISTOPHER: [*reaching into his pocket*] Would you like a truffle?
HILARY: No.
PENELOPE: It's a very expensive treat—only eaten by Russian princesses.
HILARY: Blasko says you're dangerous. The world is about to end.
CHRISTOPHER & PENELOPE: [*together*] No, no, no, no, no, no.
CHRISTOPHER: That's a far too reductive description of an extremely complicated, ultimately natural anomaly that may or may not take place in the near or distant future.
PENELOPE: What a fountain of information you are, Princess Hilary.
CHRISTOPHER: She deserves a reward.
PENELOPE: Yes, but we only have the truffle.
HILARY: Where is it?
CHRISTOPHER: Here—in my pocket. A little after-dinner treat wrapped with gold leaf and silken thread, Your Highness.
HILARY: Is it a chocolate?

PENELOPE: Much rarer than chocolate. A truffle has powers of allure.

CHRISTOPHER: In France it is known as the food of love.

HILARY: It makes people love you?

PENELOPE: Why—I believe you could have your choice of anyone at this party.

HILARY: I only want one boy—but I'm not supposed to feed you.

CHRISTOPHER & PENELOPE: [*together*] No, no, no, no, no, no, no.

CHRISTOPHER: This is completely different.

PENELOPE: We don't want food.

CHRISTOPHER: Just a small blowtorch from my toolshed.

PENELOPE: Why, we are the ones feeding you.

CHRISTOPHER: You see.

PENELOPE: We wouldn't lie to royalty.

CHRISTOPHER: Come closer.

PENELOPE: Closer.

CHRISTOPHER: Look into our eyes, Princess Hilary.

PENELOPE: Look and you will see.

CHRISTOPHER: You will see.

PENELOPE: You will look.

CHRISTOPHER: You will …

SONG: 'I CAN SEE'

CHRISTOPHER: [*singing*] 'See fields of tulips and wild apple rose'

PENELOPE: 'See pastures wide where heather grows'

CHRISTOPHER: 'See the boy you love by a river bank'

PENELOPE: 'His hair is moist and long and lank'

BOTH: 'The smile on his lips, it grows
And grows and grows—closer like destiny'

HILARY: 'I can see, I can'

BOTH: 'You can see'

HILARY: 'I can see—'

BOTH: 'She can see'

HILARY: 'I can see'

BOTH: 'Look into my eyes, look into my eyes'

CHRISTOPHER: 'See winter fires caressing your sheet'

PENELOPE: 'A soft feather bed and your naked feet'

CHRISTOPHER: 'See the boy you love, he is sleeping in'

PENELOPE: 'Spreadeagled—translucent as porcelain'
BOTH: 'A lovely boy who lives for thee
             For thee—he is your destiny'
HILARY: 'I can see, I can'
BOTH: 'You can see'
HILARY: 'I can see'
BOTH: 'She can see'
HILARY: 'I can see'
BOTH: 'Look into my eyes, look into my eyes'

SCENE TWELVE

The tennis court. SUCK-FACE *is crying.* ZACK *and* TANK *enter.* TIFFANY
is overtly ignoring HUGO.

ZACK: [*looking offstage*] Hey, you, yeah you on the balcony— [*To* TANK]
    Who is that?

TANK: Year Nines—da.

ZACK: [*looking offstage*] Put down the totem tennis pole. Stay away from
    the pool.

HUGO: They're playing totem tennis on the balcony?

TANK: Trying to pole vault over the electric fence.

ZACK: Sarah's right, this party is out of control.

HUGO: Whoa, Tiffany—what is wrong with your face, dude?

TIFFANY: I'm not staring! I'm ignoring you.

TANK: Her nose stud is infected.

ZACK: [*noticing*] Suck-face?

HUGO: Broke up with Motor-mouth.

ZACK: No way.

TANK: First sign of the apocalypse—da.

SUCK-FACE: He's probably lying in a ditch overdosing on Wizz Fizz—
    and it's all my fault.

TIFFANY: [*looking in a make-up mirror*] Oh, my God.

TANK: Just take it out, Tiffany—before they have to amputate.

ZACK: Is anyone else hungry?

HUGO: Starving.

TIFFANY: Sarah told you to find the generator.

ZACK: Do I look like an electrician?

TANK: No—you look like a guy who needs to man up.

TIFFANY: [*her nose*] *Ouch!*

ZACK: Says the girl who didn't tell anyone she has cancer.

SUCK-FACE: I can help you look.

TANK: Take Hugo.

ZACK: You three are just going to sit here.

TANK: End of the world—da.

TIFFANY: Blood poisoning—da.

SUCK-FACE: Death by Wizz Fizz! Da.

> HUGO *and* ZACK *exit.* TIFFANY *paints her toenails.*

TIFFANY: Have you and Hugo broken up?

TANK: You have to be together to break up.

TIFFANY: So, like, what—you're just using him for sex?

> SUCK-FACE *bursts into tears.*

TANK: Wow. Motor-mouth really broke her heart.

TIFFANY: [*to* SUCK-FACE] You wanna talk about it?

SUCK-FACE: I didn't mean to use him. I just needed proof.

TIFFANY: Sex doesn't prove anything.

TANK: Da. Sex is just, you know—a distraction.

SUCK-FACE: The thing is I've never been … distracted. And I think I would enjoy being distracted just once before I explode. Like, really, really, distracted.

TIFFANY: You're not seriously going to blow yourself up? Are you?

SUCK-FACE: Maybe. What about you?

TIFFANY: Hello! I'm wearing Chanel.

TANK: It's secondhand Supre—you bought it on eBay.

SUCK-FACE: But what if there really is a cosmic wormhole?

TIFFANY: I'm not merging my consciousness without a guarantee the 'me' in the next dimension has a decent wardrobe.

TANK: Why do you care so much about that stuff?

TIFFANY: Why didn't you tell me you had cancer?

SUCK-FACE: If the world is going to end none of it matters.

TIFFANY: It always matters.

TANK: [*with reluctant guilt*] The chilli pink or tangerine makes a difference if you don't have any toes left?

TIFFANY: [*angry and wounded*] The chilli pink defines me as person. Anyone who doesn't get that is kidding themselves.

SUCK-FACE: Maybe you should sue for compensation.

>   *Beat.*

TIFFANY: What do you mean?

SUCK-FACE: Well, they obviously have money. Technically she's kid-napped us.

TANK: [*too right*] Da.

SUCK-FACE: So … if you want to be rich …

TANK: [*realising*] Da.

SUCK-FACE: You could buy a whole store full of clothes.

TIFFANY: Fashion, jewellery. [*Ding*] I could start my own business.

TANK: Toenail polish.

TIFFANY: Boutique toenail polish.

SUCK-FACE: Little anklets.

TANK: Do something for the Third World.

TIFFANY: A percentage of the profit helps a starving African child.

SUCK-FACE: Everyone does the starving African child.

TANK: Something original.

TIFFANY: Toenails.

TANK: Nail polish.

SUCK-FACE: Legs. Feet.

TIFFANY: Oh, my God!

TANK & SUCK-FACE: [*together*] What?

TIFFANY: Little kiddy amputees!

TANK: Like, landmines.

SUCK-FACE: Like in the Iraqi war.

TIFFANY: Little legs blown off!

SONG: 'I CAN SEE'

TIFFANY: [*singing*] 'I see tragic orphans
>   Without any toes'

TANK: [*spoken*] The irony sucks.

TIFFANY: [*singing*] 'But the money flows'

SUCK-FACE: 'You can help them all'

TIFFANY: 'With my enterprise'

TANK: 'You can save the world'

TIFFANY: 'I can change their lives'

ALL: 'The smiles on the children

> Grow and grow and grow
> Closer like destiny—I can see'

HILARY, *with* CHRISTOPHER *and* PENELOPE *in their cage, join in.*

HILARY: 'I can see'
CHRISTOPHER
& PENELOPE: 'You can see'
ALL: 'I can see, I can see'

ZACK *appears in light.*

ZACK: 'I dream I'm standing on my roof
                 The moon is full, the wind is warm
                 The backyards stretching out as far as I can see'
HUGO: 'I'm surfing waves
                 The sky is clear, the ocean's deep and crystal blue
                 The sun is on my back'
BOTH: 'I never want to stop, I feel so free'
ALL: 'I can see'
CHRISTOPHER
& PENELOPE: 'See chocolate sundaes and sweet apple pies'
TANK, TIFFANY
& SUCK-FACE: 'See children walking'
ZACK: 'See starry skies'
SUCK-FACE
& HILARY: 'See the boy I love on a summer's day'
TIFFANY: 'See me rich and famous'
ZACK, TANK,
& HUGO: 'See me far away'
CHRISTOPHER
& PENELOPE: 'The smile on his lips'
ALL: 'It grows and grows
                 And grows closer like destiny'
CHRISTOPHER
& PENELOPE: 'Can you see?'
ALL: 'I can see'
CHRISTOPHER
& PENELOPE: 'You can see'
ALL: 'I can see, I can see'

CHRISTOPHER
& PENELOPE: 'Look into my eyes, look into my eyes'

SCENE THIRTEEN

HUGO *and* ZACK *are at the empty cage, situated behind* TANK, TIFFANY *and* SUCK-FACE. SARAH, BLASKO *and* MOTOR-MOUTH *enter.*

SARAH: Where are they?
ZACK: Don't look at me. I didn't touch it.
SARAH: I didn't say you did.
TIFFANY: What-*evah*. If you two are going to break up then just *break up*—stop ruining a moment of, like, perfect epiphany.
TANK: Did you find the generator?

    Dialogue overlaps:

HUGO: You know—I am sick of being treated like I'm just some / other guy.
MOTOR-MOUTH: Friends respect each other's feelings, in this dog-eat-dog world of instant / gratification.
SUCK-FACE: Have you been snorting Wizz / Fizz?
ZACK: Tiffany's right—I can't do this / anymore.
TANK: I'd rather blow myself up than spend another / night with you—
SARAH: What are you talking / about?
TIFFANY: Epiphany!
ZACK: This—us.
SUCK-FACE: We should never have come to this party.
MOTOR-MOUTH: Are you kidding—it's a blast. Get it? *Blast!* An allegorical pun, intended to lighten the mood of an otherwise tense situation.
ALL: Motor-mouth!
MOTOR-MOUTH: Oh, come on. All we ever hear about is hashtag-polar bear, extinction, drought, North Korea boom, Donald Trump bleh, and if all that wasn't bad enough, the girl I love is using me for sex, I'm high on Wizz Fizz, Professor Pluto's brain's in a pickle jar—I don't even have my asthma pump—and in forty-two minutes I'll be dead—so I am taking a stand! Unless, of course, I continue to hyperventilate while my CO_2 levels reach critical mass.

    He collapses.

SUCK-FACE: Motor-mouth?

HUGO: You know, he's got a point.

SUCK-FACE: Where's your extractor thingy?

MOTOR-MOUTH: Too late—blood pressure one-forty over ninety.

SARAH: He's having a panic attack.

TIFFANY: Call an ambulance.

ZACK: With what—Morse code?

SUCK-FACE: Somebody distract him with a science question.

> SUCK-FACE *is searching* MOTOR-MOUTH*'s pockets.*

TIFFANY: What star sign was Selena Gomez born under?

ZACK: Does anyone else smell fish?

SUCK-FACE: [*finding a paper bag*] He always packs an emergency sandwich.

HUGO: He doesn't look very hungry.

> MOTOR-MOUTH *breathes into the paper bag.*

SUCK-FACE: Please, Motor-mouth—you've got the rest of your life to live.

HUGO: Yeah, dude—all forty minutes of it.

> MOTOR-MOUTH *panics again.*

TIFFANY: But, like—it's not the end of the world.

> *Panic*

HUGO: Yeah, man, I mean Armageddon sucks—but look on the bright side, at least things can't get any worse, right?

> *They all half-heartedly agree.*

SONG: 'SUCK MY ARMAGEDDON'

HUGO: [*singing*] 'Who feels like catching a dose of Ebola?'

ALL: [*spoken*] Well, yeah. / Okay. / I guess so. [Et cetera]

HUGO: [*singing*] 'Who's getting diabetes drinking Coca-Cola?'

TIFFANY: 'Who's flying high on bipolar?'

HUGO: 'Who wants sex, drugs and rock and roller?'

TIFFANY: 'The wheels are stuck, baby
    On the eve of destruc—tion
    Who's getting off this truck, baby, saying
    I don't care—what the—'

ALL: [*spoken*] *Yeah, yeah, yeah!*

HUGO: 'Suck my, suck my Armageddon'
TIFFANY: 'Who wants a night they'll be regrettin'?'
HUGO: 'Who's got a thirst that's needing wettin'?'
TIFFANY: 'Who's got skin that needs sheddin'?'
ALL: [*spoken*] Yeah!
HUGO: 'Then suck my, suck my Armageddon'
TIFFANY: 'Who gives a shit if we're all in denial?'

     MOTOR-MOUTH *rallies.*

MOTOR-MOUTH: [*spoken*] If we're gonna die tonight then I am going
   in style.
HUGO: 'Who's with me, ready to spiral?
              Pass the scotch and let's turn up the dial'
TANK: 'We're in the muck, baby
              On the even of destruction but
              If we're shit out of luck, baby
              I don't care—what the—'
ALL: 'Yeah, yeah, yeah—
              Suck my, suck my Armageddon'
SARAH: 'Who's got a mood that needs resettin'?'
HUGO: 'I got a cure for all that frettin''
TANK: 'We all deserve more than we're gettin''
ZACK: 'Reset the clock and start forgettin''
TIFFANY: 'Screw all the doom and gloom and dreadin''
MOTOR-MOUTH
& SUCK-FACE: 'If the end of the world is where we're headin''
TIFFANY: 'Then suck my'
ALL: 'Suck my'
HUGO: 'Suck my'
ALL: 'Suck my'
TIFFANY
& HUGO: 'Suck my'
ALL: 'Suck my—suck my Armageddon'
SARAH: 'I'm so sick of terrorism'
TIFFANY: 'Environmentalism'
TANK: 'Consumerism'
TIFFANY: 'Mega-freaking activism'

ZACK: 'Doom-saying ultra-depressive dickheads'
SARAH: 'Spouting nihlistic wank'
SUCK-FACE: 'I could vomit an ocean of carbon dioxide
             And start my own emissions bank!'
MOTOR-MOUTH: 'Who feels like catching a dose of Ebola?'
ALL: 'Suck my Armageddon
             Suck my Armageddon
             Suck my Arma—'
SUCK-FACE: 'Getting diabetes drinking Coca-Cola?
ALL: 'Suck my Armageddon
             Suck my Armageddon
             Suck my Arma—'
HUGO: 'Who's got a thirst that's needin' wettin'?'
TIFFANY: 'Who's got skin that needs sheddin'?'
TANK: 'Then screw all this
             Doom amd gloom and dreadin'
             If the end of the world is where we're headin''
ALL: 'Suck my, suck my, suck my Armageddon'
GROUP 1:   'Suck my Armageddon, suck my, suck my'
GROUP 2:   'Ah—ah—ah—ah'
GROUP 3:   'Suck a suck a suck a suck a … [Et cetera]'
ALL: 'Armageddon!'

*A spark. Sizzle—*ZOMBIE HILARY *enters.*

SONG: 'YOU DON'T NEED TO WORRY'

HILARY: [*singing*] 'You don't need to worry
             The end of the world isn't nigh
             A solar flare's not coming
             And nobody here's
             Gonna die, die, die, die, die, die
             Would you jump off a cliff
             Just 'cause someone told you to?
             Would you blow out your brains
             Even if the worst was true?
             You don't need to escape
             Forget about intervention
             Killing yourself won't help you leap

Into the next dimension
Anyone who says that is telling a porky pie
There's no such thing as zombies
And no-one is going to—die!'

ZOMBIE HILARY *attacks* SUCK-FACE.

MOTOR-MOUTH *is thrown away.* ZACK *and* HUGO *are slammed.* SARAH *unleashes a barrage of martial arts—and is knocked to the ground.*

BLASKO *enters with a totem tennis pole. She beatboxes and dances.* HILARY *is distracted—jerking to the beatbox rhythm.*

BLASKO: Fire in the hole!

BLASKO *plunges the pole through* HILARY. MOTOR-MOUTH *grabs the other end. They pull back and forward until* ZOMBIE HILARY *is dead—for now.*

While everyone is distracted, ZOMBIE BOY *steals the brain.*

HUGO: Whoa, man, you like, disembowelled Hilary with a totem tennis pole.

BLASKO: We have to put my parents back in the cage. They can turn everyone here into mindless zombies.

ZACK: Are you out of your freaking mind?

TIFFANY: She looks like a zombie.

BLASKO: She is a zombie. Fortunately they are easily distracted by Bollywood and beatboxing—but only in the early stages.

SARAH: The bleeding has stopped.

BLASKO: Standard zombie physiology. When she wakes she will have the strength of ten men.

TIFFANY: Oh, my God—she's still breathing.

SARAH: Her heart is beating again—she's not dead.

BLASKO: Where is the brain?

ZACK: Your parents cannot turn people into zombies.

BLASKO: I left it right here.

TIFFANY: We should lock her in the cage.

BLASKO: A waste of time and energy. Gather everyone you can find. Meet me by the pool in exactly … thirty-five minutes.

SARAH: Where are you going?

BLASKO: To find Professor Pluto's brain—and drug my parents again.

SUCK-FACE: Motor-mouth?

MOTOR-MOUTH: It's alright, Suck-face, you're safe now.

ZACK: This is insane.

SARAH: It's Armageddon, Zack. You have to commit to something sooner or later.

> *All exit.* MOTOR-MOUTH *and* SUCK-FACE *are alone with* ZOMBIE HILARY.

SUCK-FACE: You murdered Hilary with a totem tennis pole—for me?

MOTOR-MOUTH: It's the least I could do when a zombified ex-girlfriend was trying to strangle you with her bare hands.

> ZOMBIE HILARY *springs to life.* MOTOR-MOUTH *and* SUCK-FACE *plunge the totem tennis pole through her.*

MOTOR-MOUTH
& SUCK-FACE: [*singing*] 'Suck my—suck my Armageddon!'

END OF ACT ONE

ACT TWO

SCENE ONE

ZOMBIE BOY *is salivating over Professor Pluto's brain in the jar.*

SONG: 'I EAT BRAINS, THEREFORE I AM'

ZOMBIE BOY: [*singing*] 'Alas, Professor Pluto, I knew him
A scientist of infinite jest
Look how his brain
Doth quiver in its juices
His frontal lobe's
A cut above the rest
Is it right that I should
Masticate such genius?
Do I bite off more than I can chew?
Why should I give a damn
I eat brains—therefore I am
But what's the meaning
In this one thing that I do?
I eat brains, therefore I am
But am I sure there isn't more?
The end is nigh yet I remain lascivious
Is it right that I would rather be oblivious?

With doomsday round the bend
Should I consume right to the end?
Will I abstain or let loose the beast
If Ghandi were a zombie
Would he starve or would he feast?

I eat brains, therefore I bite
I could be right to want to bite
We're almost cooked
Why not embrace my hunger?
We're all about to die

I'm not getting any younger
On the other hand
His brain could save the planet
Could I live with the regret
The existential threat?
And yet, and yet, and yet …
I eat brains, therefore I am
I eat brains, not pork or lamb
Should I question what I do
Oh, to chew or not to chew?
It's not hygienic, it's not glam
I'm not ashamed
Don't give a damn
I am a zombie
I eat brains, therefore I am'

CHRISTOPHER *and* PENELOPE *enter and kill* ZOMBIE BOY *with a chainsaw—and take the brain.*

CHRISTOPHER: [*spoken*] Naughty zombie.

SCENE TWO

A bathroom. TIFFANY *fights a horde of* ZOMBIES *with a toilet brush.*

SONG: 'GONNA SAVE THE WORLD'

TIFFANY: [*singing*] 'You want a piece of me, zombie
You want to eat my brain?
Whatever!
Bite me—freaking zombie

Come and feel some pain
You want to see me bleeding?
Turn me into mush—boring!
Bite me—freaking zombie
Eat my toilet brush
I'm gonna

The ZOMBIES *creep towards her.*

ALL: 'She's gonna'

TIFFANY:	'I'm gonna save the world
	You can't break me
	You won't shake me'
ALL:	'She's gonna save the world'
TIFFANY:	'Got a vision to go far
	Seen the future, I'm a star'
ALL:	'Star'
TIFFANY:	'A star—a star!

TIFFANY *fights back.*

You want to feast on me, zombie?
Come on if you dare
Hasta la vista!
You want me? Come and get me
I'm not going anywhere
You want to see me splattered?
See my innards gush
Whatever!
Slow down, you freaking psychos
What's the freaking rush!
I have to'

ALL:	'She has to'
TIFFANY:	'I have to change the world
	You won't beat me
	You can't eat me'
ALL:	'She has to change the world'
TIFFANY:	'Got a reason to go far
	Save the kiddies—be a'
ALL:	'Star, a star, a star'

TIFFANY *escapes.*

SCENE THREE

Meanwhile, in the dining room, HUGO *and* TANK *sit in awkward silence.*

HUGO: The house is quiet.
TANK: Too quiet—da.
HUGO: Want to play table tennis?

TANK: I hate table tennis.

HUGO: You wouldn't say that if you were Chinese.

TANK: Maybe the world is already over.

HUGO: It will be if Tiffany doesn't [*calling out*] hurry up with the nachos!

TANK: You let her wander around a house full of zombies.

HUGO: One freaking zombie. Besides, she wanted to go.

TANK: She really likes you, Hugo.

HUGO: I'm not going to feel responsible just because she likes me. Look, I'm sorry I told her about your cancer.

TANK: Whatever. In twenty minutes who gives a shit.

HUGO: You going to blow yourself up?

TANK: None of your freaking business.

HUGO: We could do it together.

TANK: Da.

HUGO: I never told Tiffany about us. I wanted to.

TANK: It was one night.

HUGO: You can't pretend it never happened.

TANK: I can for another twenty minutes.

HUGO: So what—you're ashamed?

TANK: You don't love me, Hugo, you don't even like me, cancer is a turn-on for you.

HUGO: So it makes you interesting.

> TIFFANY *enters, out of breath, waving the toilet brush.* TANK *exits.*

TIFFANY: Hugo.

HUGO: Tiffany, dude, ah, listen—I want apologise for the nachos, you know, the whole, risk your life 'cause I needed time alone with Tank thing. Oh, and I'm sorry I'm not into you, okay, it's nothing personal, it's just, well—you got this whole shallow, kind of fake vibe, which is not really my scene. But who knows, right, maybe in the other dimension.

> *He chases after* TANK.

TIFFANY: Seriously!

> *The* ZOMBIES *close in again.*

>> [*Singing*] 'You want to cut me down, zombie
>> Want to rip out my heart'

[*Spoken*] Take a number!
> [*Singing*] 'Up yours, freaking zombie
> You won't tear this girl apart
> Want to see me gutted
> Crying out in shame?'

[*Spoken*] Bring it on, mister!
> [*Singing*] 'Screw you, freaking zombie
> And don't forget my name
> 'Cause I'm gonna'

ALL: 'She's gonna'
TIFFANY: 'I'm gonna save the world
>   You can't break me
>   You won't shake me'
ALL: 'She's gonna save the world'
TIFFANY: 'Got a vision to go far
>   Seen the future, I'm a star—'
ALL: 'Star'
TIFFANY: [*spoken*] I am not shallow and fake.

> *A* ZOMBIE *growl.*

Okay, so I was shallow and fake, whatever! Nobody's perfect.
ALL: [*singing*] 'Star'
TIFFANY: Oh, and just for the record—I chose to be shallow and fake, which means I am not stupid—
ALL: [*singing*] 'Star'
TIFFANY: The whole world is shallow and fake—I was just trying to keep up.
ALL: [*singing*] 'Star'
TIFFANY: I don't want be that person anymore.
ALL: [*singing*] 'Star'
TIFFANY: I've got little kiddies to save …
ALL: [*singing*] 'Star'
TIFFANY: I want to be …
ALL: [*singing*] 'Famous, compassionate, brave'
TIFFANY: 'I'm gonna save the world!'

> TIFFANY *escapes.*

SCENE FOUR

Meanwhile on the tennis court. ZACK *is running away from* SARAH.

SARAH: Zack.

ZACK: Go back to the house.

SARAH: What is wrong with you?

ZACK: I'm looking for the generator. That's what you want, right? To find the generator.

SARAH: If you don't love me—just say it.

ZACK: You don't want love—you want everything.

SARAH: What's that supposed to mean?

SONG: 'THE OTHER YOU AND ME'

ZACK: [*singing*] 'It's too late to do this now
Forget what I said—let's just pretend
I don't know what I'm saying
I mean, freaking hell—the world's about to end
So even if love you
With the heat of a supernova
It's pointless now—this dimension
This you—this me—we're over'

SARAH: 'But what if the wormhole is real
We set our consciousness free?
Merge with our other-dimensional selves
See all the things that they see?
If we get a second chance
Okay, so there's no guarantee
But could they be in love?
The other you and me?'

HUGO *appears.*

HUGO: 'You say that you know my heart
But I'm not the guy you think you know

What's the point of lying?

I mean, freaking hell
The whole world's about to blow

I'm saying that I love you
And I know you won't want to hear it
But it's the truth—I can't hide it
Oh boy—am I—in deep shit'

ZACK: 'You know what I'm trying to say'
SARAH: 'Then why can't you say what you mean?
We're going to die—you don't have to lie
Stop running away and come clean
If we get a second chance
I don't need a guarantee
I only need the truth
Could they be in love?
The other you and me?'

ZACK: 'Maybe'
SARAH: 'Maybe?'
ZACK: 'Maybe this is all just fate'
HUGO: 'This is all just fate'
ZACK: 'And maybe'
SARAH: 'Maybe?'
ZACK: 'In the other dimension
What we have is great'
HUGO: 'What we have is great'
ZACK: 'And maybe'
SARAH: 'Maybe?'
ZACK: 'We just have to wait
'Cause right now—I don't know what I feel'
HUGO
& SARAH: 'I know what I feel'
ZACK: 'Right now I don't know what is real'
HUGO
& SARAH: 'I know what is real'
ZACK: 'Right now all I know is—
It's too late to talk it out'
HUGO: 'It's not too late'
SARAH: 'It's not too late
You don't have to run away'
ZACK: 'Forget what I said, let's just pretend'

HUGO:	'Let's not pretend'
SARAH:	'If we're breaking up
	I just need to hear you say'
ZACK:	'I don't know what I'm saying'
HUGO:	'I know what I'm saying
	Before the world's about to end'
ZACK:	'I mean, freaking hell
	The whole world's about to end'
HUGO:	'I love you'
SARAH:	'Do you love me?'
ZACK:	'I don't know what I feel
	I don't know if I love you
	In this dimension—or for eternity'
SARAH:	'Just tell me, could they be?'
HUGO:	'Could we be?'
ZACK:	'I don't know'
SARAH:	'Just tell me, could they be?'
HUGO:	'Could we be?'
ZACK:	'I don't know'
SARAH:	'Could they be, could they be?'
HUGO:	'Could we be?'
ZACK:	'Okay—maybe they could be in love

SARAH *reaches for* ZACK—*he steps away.*

The other you and me'

ZACK *exits.* BLASKO *enters, having overheard.*

BLASKO: Leave him, Sarah.

SARAH: He's afraid.

BLASKO: His soul is young. Yours is old. You are beautiful, Sarah. Honest. Brave. If we were in Paris at the top of the Eiffel Tower—I would look into your eyes, see a galaxy of passion exploding with starlight, and fall hopelessly in love with you.

Beat.

SARAH: You would?

BLASKO: Oh yes. But that's not important right now. What's important is to locate Professor Pluto's brain, so he can invent his solar panel in the next dimension and save the planet.

SARAH: Yes. No. Wait. You lost the brain?

BLASKO: Search the garden. I'll check the house. Remember to meet me by the pool—

SARAH: When the last polar bear dies at midnight.

BLASKO: [*impressed*] You've been paying attention. Now—go, go, go, go.

TIFFANY *enters, breathless, just as* SARAH *exits.*

TIFFANY: Sarah!

BLASKO: Ah, student two-three-two, I see you found a weapon.

TIFFANY: It's a toilet brush.

BLASKO: Do you know how to use a chainsaw?

TIFFANY: I watch *The Walking Dead*.

BLASKO: Better stick with the toilet brush.

BLASKO *exits.*

TIFFANY: No. Wait. Blasko. Sarah. Somebody, please …
                [*Singing*] 'I have to'
ALL: 'She has to'
TIFFANY: 'I have to save the world
                You won't beat me
                You can't eat me'
ALL: 'She has to save the world'
TIFFANY: 'Got a reason to go far
                Save the kiddies, be a star'
ALL: 'Star'

TIFFANY: [*spoken*] I'm sick of lying and pretending.

ALL: [*singing*] 'Star'

TIFFANY: I want a second chance …

ALL: [*singing*] 'Star'

TIFFANY: Please let me be somebody … please …

ALL: [*singing*] 'Star'

TIFFANY: I don't want to die.

PENELOPE *and* CHRISTOPHER *approach.*

PENELOPE: Well, of course you don't.

CHRISTOPHER: You must never give up hope.

TIFFANY: So, like, I'm not going to become a zombie?

PENELOPE & CHRISTOPHER: [*together*] No, no, no, no, no, no—

CHRISTOPHER: That is a far too simplistic representation of an otherwise complex and highly specialised form of social manipulation.

PENELOPE: Just look into our eyes.

CHRISTOPHER: Look and you will see.

PENELOPE: You will look.

CHRISTOPHER: You will …

PENELOPE: [*singing*] 'Become a hero'

CHRISTOPHER: 'See yourself in your own private chopper'

PENELOPE: 'The crowd below cheers'

BOTH: 'You give them a wave'

TIFFANY: 'I'm gonna save the world'

> TIFFANY *is consumed by* ZOMBIES. *Mayhem.*

SCENE FIVE

PENELOPE *and* CHRISTOPHER *do a little song and dance.*

SONG: 'AH, AH—ARAMAGEDDON'

BOTH: [*spoken, sensual*] Ah, ah, ah, *ah!*

> *Segueing into …*

[*Singing*] 'Ah—ah—ah—Armageddon
Fun for all the family
Ah—ah—ah—Armageddon
Ninety-nine percent fat free'

CHRISTOPHER: 'It's painless'

PENELOPE: 'You'll weigh less'

BOTH: 'Full of minerals and vitamin D'

CHRISTOPHER: 'Fast-working'

PENELOPE: 'And nutritious'

BOTH: 'Prevents tooth decay permanently!
Ah—ah—ah—Armageddon
Try—you'll be a whole new you
Ah—ah—ah—Armageddon
Comes in chocolate and peppermint too'

CHRISTOPHER: 'It's organic'

PENELOPE: 'Biodynamic'

BOTH: 'Carbon-neutral, worth every cent'

CHRISTOPHER: 'It's sustainable'
PENELOPE: 'Biodegradable'
BOTH: 'Good for you
                    And for the environment
                    Ah—ah—ah—Armageddon
                    Ninety-nine percent fat free
                    Ah—ah—ah—Armageddon
                    Look into my eyes, can you see?
                    Ah, look into my eye
                    Ah, look into my eyes'

ZOMBIES. *Screaming. Mayhem.*

SCENE SIX

Meanwhile. MOTOR-MOUTH *and* SUCK-FACE *are in a bedroom—standing guard against zombies. He is armed with a calculator and wears the Electro-Magnetic Anxiety Extractor on his head. She brandishes the totem tennis pole.*

MOTOR-MOUTH: Stay away from the windows and doors, Suck-face.
SUCK-FACE: If one zombie lays a finger on you, I'll rip its guts out.
MOTOR-MOUTH: And I'll stab it to death with this scientific calculator.
SUCK-FACE: Motor-mouth.
MOTOR-MOUTH: Yes, Suck-face?
SUCK-FACE: I'm sorry you don't feel loved.
MOTOR-MOUTH: I'm sorry you don't feel desired. But even though we're still virgins, trapped in this bedroom, surrounded by a horde of zombies, I just want you to know …

SONG: 'I'M SO HAPPY I COULD DIE'

                    [*Singing*] 'I'm so happy I could die
                    And, baby, you're the reason why
                    My pulmonary valves are pumping
                    My cerebral cortex cells are jumping
                    You're the reason I can fly
                    You're my dynamite—you blow me higher
                    Than a lunar module over the moon

My testicles are tingling
Not a moment too soon
Because I love you—so happy am I …
That in fifteen minutes—and twenty seconds
I could die
I'm so giddy I could trip'
SUCK-FACE: 'Take a ride with you and lose my grip'
MOTOR-MOUTH: 'Knowing that I have your affection'
SUCK-FACE: 'Now that I've experienced true perfection'
BOTH: 'I could kiss this world goodbye'
MOTOR-MOUTH: 'And not a single tear I'd cry'
SUCK-FACE: 'With your hand in mine I'll never look back'
BOTH: 'Together for eternity in our love shack'
MOTOR-MOUTH: 'Because you love me—so happy am I
             That in fourteen minutes—and twenty seconds
             I could die'

> MOTOR-MOUTH *and* SUCK-FACE *get raunchier—a weird, geeky*
> *mating ritual.*

SUCK-FACE: 'Why do I feel so strong?'
MOTOR-MOUTH: 'Because love lifts us up where we belong'
SUCK-FACE: 'How come this feels so right?'
MOTOR-MOUTH: 'It was meant to be, baby
             Tonight's our night'
BOTH: 'We're so hot we could explode
             We're on fire, baby—lock and load'
MOTOR-MOUTH: 'I never want to lose you again
             Not in this or any other dimension'
BOTH: 'The end is nigh, who cares why'
MOTOR-MOUTH: 'So happy am I
             That in thirteen minutes—and twenty seconds
             I could—'
BOTH: 'Die, [*becoming orgasmic*] die, die, die!'

> ZOMBIE HILARY *interrupts their geeky foreplay and attacks*
> SUCK-FACE. BLASKO *comes to the rescue with a power drill and*
> *kills* ZOMBIE HILARY.

BLASKO: *Clear!*

> *Beat.*

Am I interrupting something?

SUCK-FACE: Well, now that you mention it.

BLASKO: Good. Because we need to find Professor Pluto's brain immediately.

MOTOR-MOUTH: I thought you said it was in a pickle jar next to the bomb.

BLASKO: Why would I say it was in a pickle jar next to the bomb? If I knew it was in a pickle jar next to the bomb I wouldn't be interrupting the two of you attempting sexual intercourse in front of this mutilated zombie.

MOTOR-MOUTH: I was referring to your voicemail message.

BLASKO: What voicemail message?

SUCK-FACE: The one telling us where the brain would be.

BLASKO: I don't remember leaving you a voicemail message.

MOTOR-MOUTH: That's because you didn't make the phone call.

SUCK-FACE: Or send the text message.

BLASKO: What text message?

MOTOR-MOUTH: The text message with the list of items.

BLASKO: You're saying I sent you a text message with a list of items—I didn't send—followed by a voicemail message—from a phone call I didn't make—telling you the brain was in a pickle jar next to the bomb.

SUCK-FACE: Yes.

MOTOR-MOUTH: And no.

BLASKO: You do realise we only have twelve minutes before Armageddon.

SUCK-FACE: The Blasko from the dimension 'before' this dimension made the phone call.

MOTOR-MOUTH: And sent the text.

BLASKO: Wait a minute. You're saying the 'me' from the dimension 'before' this dimension sent you the text message with a list of items, followed by the voicemail message, telling you the brain was in a pickle jar next to the bomb.

MOTOR-MOUTH & SUCK-FACE: [*calculating, then together*] … Yes.

BLASKO: I don't understand. Why would I send *you* a message when I could send *me* a message? Do you have the list?

MOTOR-MOUTH: It self-destructed in sixty seconds.

BLASKO: Of course. I didn't want my parents to intercept it.

SUCK-FACE: We remembered the superglue.

BLASKO: Superglue?

They hand it to BLASKO.

MOTOR-MOUTH: Superglue was definitely on the list.

SUCK-FACE: [*also on the list*] A set of screwdrivers, a welding iron, the 'what-cha-ma-call-it-brainwave-thingy'.

MOTOR-MOUTH: You also wrote something about guns.

BLASKO: Guns!

SUCK-FACE: Magnum 45s—does that ring a bell?

BLASKO: Hmmm. Guns and superglue. Superglue and guns. Interesting. But not important right now. You—find the brain and keep it safe. I will stop my parents before it's too late.

MOTOR-MOUTH: Actually, there is one other thing we need to do first.

BLASKO: Is it more important than cosmic annihilation?

Beat.

SUCK-FACE: Well …

BLASKO: Excellent. Meet me by the pool in exactly twelve minutes to send Professor Pluto's consciousness through the wormhole.

She mimes the bomb / consciousness / wormhole et cetera—then exits—with the totem tennis pole.

SUCK-FACE: Does a brain without a body even have a consciousness?

MOTOR-MOUTH: The odds are a million to one.

SUCK-FACE: Which means the knowledge it contains about his solar panel—

MOTOR-MOUTH: Will never be transferred to his other-dimensional brain.

SUCK-FACE: He'll never finish his invention and save the planet.

MOTOR-MOUTH: Not before he dies in a bathtub race.

SUCK-FACE: There must be something we're missing.

MOTOR-MOUTH: Superglue. Guns.

SUCK-FACE: Maybe there's a way to extract the knowledge then send it through the wormhole.

MOTOR-MOUTH: It would require extensive surgery. Either that or an electro-magnetic device to regenerate his brainwaves, extract the knowledge—transfer it to a living brain—then blow that person up when the wormhole opens.

SUCK-FACE: Like when you transferred your brainwaves into my anaconda.

MOTOR-MOUTH: Exactly.

SUCK-FACE: You think that's why she told us to bring your 'what-cha-ma-call-it'?

> BLASKO *reappears in light, singing the same song—but in a different reality to* MOTOR-MOUTH *and* SUCK-FACE.

SONG: 'WELCOME TO MY PARTY'—REPRISE

BLASKO: [*singing*] 'Welcome to my party'

MOTOR-MOUTH
& SUCK-FACE: 'Gonna die'

BLASKO: 'The party to end all parties'

MOTOR-MOUTH
& SUCK-FACE: 'Say goodbye'

MOTOR-MOUTH: 'If we want to stay alive'

SUCK-FACE: 'We use your thingy to survive
            Transfer his brainwaves into you and we'll be'

ALL: 'On our way
            The part-ay to end all parties'

SCENE SEVEN

Meanwhile in the garden. TANK *pummels a lawnmower into a* ZOMBIE, *trapped under the blades.* HUGO *has a leaf blower.*

HUGO: Cut off its head.

TANK: What?

HUGO: Zombies can't come back to life if you cut off their head.

TANK: I ran out of petrol.

HUGO: Use this.

TANK: How am I supposed to kill it with a leaf blower?

HUGO: Stick it in its mouth.

TANK: I'm not touching its mouth.

HUGO: Pump it full of hot air till it explodes.

TANK: It's a zombie—not a beachball.

> ZOMBIE TIFFANY *raises a toilet brush.*

Oh, my God.

HUGO: What?

TANK: This zombie is Tiffany.

HUGO: No way.

TANK: *Da!*

HUGO: It can't be, man—I left her in the house with a toilet brush.

TANK: That toilet brush?

HUGO: Yeah! No. Wait. Let's not jump to any conclusions. I mean maybe, this zombie murdered Tiffany then stole her toilet brush.

TANK: Its nail polish is chilli pink.

HUGO: Whoa—man—positive identification.

TANK: I murdered Tiffany with a lawnmower.

HUGO: Don't be on hard on yourself, okay—these things happen.

TANK She's dead.

HUGO: She'll get over it.

> *Beat.*

She's a zombie.

TANK: Don't touch me.

HUGO: I'm trying to help.

TANK: You're a selfish, stupid, asshole.

HUGO: I know! But can I say one thing in my defence? I care about you—and I, I, I, I don't want you to blow yourself up.

TANK: What have I got to lose, Hugo? Maybe there's something better on the other side of that wormhole. Maybe I don't have cancer—da.

HUGO: So, like, you're not scared of dying?

TANK: I've had a long time to think about it. A billion stars make up a galaxy, a billion galaxies make up a universe. It's got to mean something, right?

HUGO: Right, right—and, and—I think that's what I'm trying to say, you know, because … I'm terrified of dying. But when I'm with you it doesn't matter.

> TANK *retreats.*

I know, I know I suck at explaining myself, but if this really is my last night on earth then screw Pink Floyd. I … I need you to be my last song …

SONG: 'HEART, BE A RADIO'

TANK: [*singing*] 'Heart, be a radio
           After I'm gone
           Keep playing my soul
           Let me live on
           Send me in stereo
           'Cross the galaxy
           Though the nothingness
           Of infinity—I'll go
           Until I disappear'
HUGO: 'Heart, be a radio'
TANK: 'Will somebody hear?'
HUGO: 'Heart, be a radio'
TANK: 'If I'm crystal clear'
HUGO: 'Play me in stereo'
TANK: 'Will they feel me near?'
HUGO: 'Heart, be a radio'
TANK: 'Eyes like a telescope
           Help me to see
           After I'm gone
           What will I be?
           Telescope, can you show
           Immortality
           In the emptiness?
           Is there clarity?
           Do we glow?

      SARAH *and* ZACK *enter.*

           Will I shine at night?'
HUGO, ZACK
& SARAH: 'Heart, be a radio'
TANK: 'Will they feel my light?'
HUGO, ZACK
& SARAH: 'Heart, be a radio'
TANK: 'Will they think of me?'
HUGO, ZACK
& SARAH: 'Play me in stereo'

TANK: 'For eternity?'
HUGO, ZACK
& SARAH: 'Heart, be a radio'
TANK: 'Are we moonbeams and particles
            Floating above?
            Stardust and memories
            Photons of love?
            Don't want to disappear'
HUGO, ZACK
& SARAH: 'Heart, be a radio'
TANK: 'Want someone to hear'
HUGO, ZACK
& SARAH: 'Heart, be a radio'
TANK: 'Play me loud in cars'
HUGO, ZACK
& SARAH: 'Play me in stereo'
TANK: 'Strum me on guitars'
HUGO, ZACK
& SARAH: 'Heart, be a radio'
TANK: 'Is there life on Mars?'
HUGO, ZACK
& SARAH: 'Heart, be a radio'

ZOMBIES *attack* TANK *and* HUGO. ZACK *and* SARAH *escape.*
PENELOPE *and* CHRISTOPHER *revel in the chaos.*

SONG: 'AH, AH—ARMAGEDDON—LIFE GOES ON'

PENELOPE
& CHRISTOPHER: [*singing*] 'Ah—ah—ah—Armageddon
            Try it just the once—you'll see
            Ah—ah—ah—Armageddon
            Nature's own remedy'
CHRISTOPHER: 'It's economical'
PENELOPE: 'Quick and practical'
BOTH: 'Progress with a capital "P"'
CHRISTOPHER: 'It's revolutionary'
PENELOPE: 'It's evolutionary'
BOTH: 'Extinction is just another opportunity!'

The ZOMBIES—TANK, ZOMBIE BOY, HILARY, HUGO *and* TIFFANY—*join in the song.*

CHRISTOPHER: [*spoken*] You see, boys and girls, there are those in the world who say Armageddon is bad for you.

PENELOPE: Silly people—outrageous people.

CHRISTOPHER: You must not let them win, noooo—

PENELOPE: You must thrive while the opportunity presents itself, after all …

ZOMBIES: [*singing*] 'Life goes on!'

PENELOPE: Three words that sum up the great truth of the universe …

ZOMBIES: [*singing*] 'Life goes on!'

CHRISTOPHER: Yes, the equator will heat up a little.

PENELOPE: Hurricanes will blow a little, but …

ZOMBIES: [*singing*] 'Life goes on!'

PENELOPE: Oceans rise a little.

CHRISTOPHER: Small Pacific islands sink a little, but …

ZOMBIES: [*singing*] 'Life goes on!'

PENELOPE: Bushfires burn a little.

CHRISTOPHER: Polar bears on little icebergs die a little, but …

ZOMBIES: [*singing*] 'Life goes on!'

CHRISTOPHER: Yes! Global warming will magnify the solar flare, ending all life on earth.

PENELOPE: But planetary annihilation never *really* hurt anybody.

BOTH: No, no, no, no, no.

PENELOPE: Like ripping off a bandaid.

CHRISTOPHER: The second it's all over.

PENELOPE: Somewhere …

CHRISTOPHER: Somehow …

PENELOPE: Even if it's just a little virus …

CHRISTOPHER: On a little chunk of rock that used to be the earth …

ZOMBIES: [*singing*] 'Life goes on!'

SCENE EIGHT

BLASKO *discovers her parents—she has the totem tennis pole.* ZOMBIE BOY *seizes the opportunity and steals back the brain—before anyone notices.*

BLASKO: Mother, father!

CHRISTOPHER & PENELOPE: [*together*] Blasko!

BLASKO: Stop turning my friends into mindless zombies.

CHRISTOPHER: No-one is blowing themselves up, young lady.

PENELOPE: A cosmic wormhole is not a toy.

CHRISTOPHER: It is a very valuable piece of classified information.

BLASKO: I am taking them with me.

PENELOPE: Blasko, be reasonable, you cannot bring these children into the next dimension.

CHRISTOPHER: Like releasing a pet rabbit into the wild.

PENELOPE: They would suffer.

CHRISTOPHER: Make lots of other little rabbits.

PENELOPE: They cannot be trusted with something as important as the future of the planet.

CHRISTOPHER: Or Professor Pluto's brain. Although, we must admit, the idea of sending his consciousness through the cosmic wormhole—

PENELOPE: Impressive.

CHRISTOPHER: Audacious.

PENELOPE: And extremely irresponsible.

PENELOPE: Much better to let nature take its course.

BLASKO: I know what you did to me in the dimensions before this one.

> *Beat.*

CHRISTOPHER: I beg your pardon?

PENELOPE: We didn't 'do' anything.

BLASKO: Stop lying.

BOTH: No, no, no, no, no, no, no—

PENELOPE: We're not lying.

CHRISTOPHER: We're just confused by the ambiguity of your statement and don't wish to incriminate ourselves until absolutely necessary.

BLASKO: How many times have I thrown this party?

PENELOPE: Well, let's see—there was the dimension when you locked us in the sauna.

CHRISTOPHER: And replaced the steam with laughing gas.

PENELOPE: [*laughing*] Wonderful, oh, and the dimension when she used grenades to bury us in the basement.

CHRISTOPHER: Ingenious! Oh, oh—let's not forget the dimension when she tied us to that hot air balloon then flew us all the way to Tasmania.

PENELOPE: Extraordinary.

CHRISTOPHER: Inspiring.

PENELOPE: Then just when we thought we'd seen it all …

CHRISTOPHER: [*extreme pride*] Sleeping pills in our salmon mousse.

BLASKO: Yes—but—how many times have I succeeded?

PENELOPE: Interesting question.

CHRISTOPHER: Define success.

BLASKO: How many times have I sent Professor Pluto's brain through the wormhole? How many times did I save the planet?

CHRISTOPHER: Well, technically speaking …

PENELOPE: None.

CHRISTOPHER: But don't be hard on yourself. Extinction is like puberty. Highly emotional.

PENELOPE: Eventually things settle down.

CHRISTOPHER: You get taller. Bits of you expand.

PENELOPE: It's a journey to maturity.

BLASKO: I don't understand. Are you saying you have never let me through the wormhole?

CHRISTOPHER: Well, of course not.

PENELOPE: Don't be ridiculous.

CHRISTOPHER: You're dangerous enough now.

PENELOPE: You would be out of control if we let your consciousness into the next dimension.

BLASKO: You leave me behind to die.

CHRISTOPHER: Now, Blasko—we do not lay guilt trips in this family.

PENELOPE: Besides, there are plenty more dimensions where you are alive and well.

BLASKO: But I want to make a difference. I want to change at least one world for the better.

CHRISTOPHER: Which is a perfectly normal phase to go through.

PENELOPE: We all get the urge at one time or another.

CHRISTOPHER: Why, when I was your age—I was quite the rebel.

　　　Beat.

BLASKO: You mean—you have experienced these feelings too?

BOTH: Absolutely. / Oh my, yes—

PENELOPE: You're idealism is commendable.

CHRISTOPHER: Compassionate.

PENELOPE: Just not practical.

BLASKO: But—don't you see? We could change the world together.

PENELOPE: Into what?

Beat.

BLASKO: Something different.

CHRISTOPHER: You'll have to be a little more specific.

PENELOPE: What would you change, Blasko?

CHRISTOPHER: What does your new world look like?

BLASKO: I … I haven't solved that part—but …

PENELOPE: But …

BLASKO: I need …

PENELOPE: Meaning?

CHRISTOPHER: Certainty.

PENELOPE: You feel alone.

BLASKO: I feel very alone.

PENELOPE: We understand, you see.

CHRISTOPHER: That is why family is so important.

Beat.

BLASKO: I'm sorry I drugged your salmon mousse.

PENELOPE: Growing up isn't easy.

CHRISTOPHER: Who knows, perhaps this time things can turn out differently.

BLASKO: You would take me with you?

PENELOPE: Of course, if you're ready. Just put down the totem tennis pole.

CHRISTOPHER: We'll turn the rest of your friends into mindless zombies.

PENELOPE: Wait for the wormhole to open.

CHRISTOPHER: Then blow out each other's brains.

PENELOPE: Painlessly.

CHRISTOPHER: Instantaneously. With our specially engraved Magnum 45s.

PENELOPE: We love you, Blasko.

SONG: *'I AM NOT YOU'*

BLASKO: [*singing*] 'Mother, father

I love you both too
Your words are convincing
And yes, they ring true
I want to be family
To feel like a team
It's like I've been dreaming
A very strange dream
You're right—I should wake up
But what do I do
If this is just me
And I'm not like you?

Mother, father
I hear what you say
There's reason and logic
And choices to weigh
But what if I'm right and what if you're wrong?
I don't want to fight, but should I stay strong?
Perhaps I need purpose to act and to do
A reason to live
If I'm not like you'

PENELOPE: 'It's not about right or wrong'
CHRISTOPHER: 'It's simply reality'
PENELOPE: 'You'll feel better tomorrow'
CHRISTOPHER
& PENELOPE: 'Just wait and see'
BLASKO: 'No'
CHRISTOPHER
& PENELOPE: 'See'
BLASKO: 'No—I know what you're trying to do
     Mother, father
     I love you, I do
     A change has been coming
     It's long overdue
     Don't be angry or hurt
     Give it time to sink in
     Then do what you must

Let the best Tupper win
Yes, I am your daughter
I'm my own person too
We'll always be family
But I'm not like you'

BLASKO *exits.*

PENELOPE & CHRISTOPHER: [*spoken, together*] Blasko!

SCENE NINE

The pool. ZOMBIE BOY *prepares a picnic for himself. The brain in the pickle jar. A small rug. A knife and fork. He tucks the 'fishpaste letter' under his chin—like a napkin. He is about to feast when ...* SUCK-FACE *enters with a chainsaw and cuts him down.*

SUCK-FACE: *Clear!*

MOTOR-MOUTH *takes the brain—and they exit just as* ZOMBIE HILARY *enters, sniffing for their scent.* ZOMBIE BOY *comes back to life. He looks for the brain—then—zing!—discovers the girl of his dreams chewing on her own arm.*

SONG: 'A BRAIN MADE FOR TWO'

ZOMBIE BOY: [*singing*] 'If I looked her way
　　　　　　　　Would she steal a glance?
　　　　　　　　Could we even share a zombie dance?
　　　　　　　　All the things that we could do
　　　　　　　　With a brain that's made for two'
HILARY:　　　'If I smiled at him
　　　　　　　　Would he see me blush?
　　　　　　　　I might have no pulse
　　　　　　　　He can't feel it rush
　　　　　　　　But my heart could still be true
　　　　　　　　With a brain that's made for two'
ZOMBIE BOY: 'If I bared my soul would she only scoff?'
HILARY:　　　'Would he hold my hand if it fell right off?'
ZOMBIE BOY: 'Would she stir my zombie loins with her kiss?
　　　　　　　　Could she love me for my rotting flesh

And stubborn rigor mortis?'

Music. The ZOMBIES *dance as* MOTOR-MOUTH *places the Electro-Magnetic Brainwave Anxiety Extractor over his head.* SUCK-FACE *connects it to Professor Pluto's pickle jar with a series of wires.*

MOTOR-MOUTH: Extractor on head, check?

SUCK-FACE: Check.

MOTOR-MOUTH: Pickle jar secure, check?

SUCK-FACE: Check. Are you sure we should be plugging you into the electric fence without a proper risk assessment?

MOTOR-MOUTH: It's the only way to generate the required voltage.

SUCK-FACE: What if you pass out and hit your head again?

MOTOR-MOUTH: Blood pressure: one-ten over ninety—heart rate stable.

SUCK-FACE: You're being so … brave.

MOTOR-MOUTH: Am I? I am. Well, I mean, the future of the world is at stake. But don't forget. To transfer Professor Pluto's knowledge into *my* brain, we have to reverse the polarity.

SUCK-FACE: Green button.

MOTOR-MOUTH: Correct.

SUCK-FACE: What happens if I press the red button?

MOTOR-MOUTH: My nervous system will overload and the pickle jar will develop a stutter. Check?

SUCK-FACE: Check.

MOTOR-MOUTH: Commence transfer in T-minus—three, two—

SUCK-FACE: Wait. There's something I want to say in case I never get the chance to say it again.

MOTOR-MOUTH: And I want to say, you don't have to say anything that makes you feel uncomfortable.

SUCK-FACE: I want to say thank you for not making me feel stupid.

MOTOR-MOUTH: [*disappointed*] Oh. I see.

SUCK-FACE: I mean, let's face it—you're so smart and I'm … not.

MOTOR-MOUTH: You surf the dark web and hack the CIA.

SUCK-FACE: That's not the same.

MOTOR-MOUTH: It is to me.

Pause.

Suck-face.

SUCK-FACE: Yes, Motor-mouth.

MOTOR-MOUTH: I love you.

SUCK-FACE: Motor-mouth.

MOTOR-MOUTH: Yes, Suck-face?

SUCK-FACE: We have four minutes and twenty seconds till the wormhole opens.

ZOMBIE BOY
& HILARY: [*singing*] 'Could you really be the one for me
    With your skin so pale
    And your breath so stale?
    Could this love be true
    With a brain made just for …'

SUCK-FACE: [*spoken*] Three—

ZOMBIE BOY & HILARY: [*singing*] 'Two—'

MOTOR-MOUTH: [*spoken*] One—

SUCK-FACE: Contact!

> SUCK-FACE *hits the green button.* BLASKO *kills* ZOMBIE BOY *and* ZOMBIE HILARY *with the power drill. The electric fence sizzles. The extractor lights up—transference takes place.*

Oh no. I think we blew a fuse.

BLASKO: What are you doing with Professor Pluto?

SUCK-FACE: Transferring his consciousness to Motor-mouth's brain.

BLASKO: Wait a minute. Did the other me think of that?

SUCK-FACE: Yes—but we had to use the electric fence as a power source.

BLASKO: Did you reconfigure the voltage?

SUCK-FACE: I pressed the green button.

> MOTOR-MOUTH's *body is dancing the macarena.*

BLASKO: Professor Pluto, are you in there?

SUCK-FACE: Speak to me, Motor-mouth.

BLASKO: Perhaps the transfer is affecting his neural pathways. Either that or he's dancing the macarena.

SUCK-FACE: Motor-mouth! Motor-mouth, can you hear me?

> BLASKO *notices Professor Pluto's brain is flashing wildly.*

BLASKO: Ask him again.

SUCK-FACE: Motor-mouth! If you can hear, give me a sign.

BLASKO: Tell him to blink three times.

SUCK-FACE: I need you to blink three times if you can hear me.

The pickle jar with the brain flashes three times.

BLASKO: [*realising*] The power surge must have overloaded the circuits.

The jar is blinking wildly.

SUCK-FACE: Oh no—you don't mean that—

BLASKO: Blink three more times if Professor Pluto is in there with you.

The pickle jar flashes three times.

SUCK-FACE: I transferred Motor-mouth into a pickle jar.

BLASKO: The good news is we have proof they are both conscious. Now we just wait for the wormhole to open and blow them up!

> PENELOPE *and* CHRISTOPHER *enter and take hold of* MOTOR-MOUTH.

PENELOPE & CHRISTOPHER: [*together*] Blasko!

BLASKO: [*to* SUCK-FACE] Take the brain to the beachball. Go!

> SUCK-FACE *escapes.* ZACK *and* SARAH *enter, pursued by* ZOMBIES.

PENELOPE: We know what you're trying to do.

CHRISTOPHER: Transferring Professor Pluto's consciousness to a living body.

PENELOPE: Extraordinary.

CHRISTOPHER: Ingenious.

PENELOPE: But we cannot allow you to save the planet in the next dimension.

> ZACK *and* SARAH *are being overwhelmed by* ZOMBIES.

ZACK: Get out while you still can, Sarah.

SARAH: I'm not going anywhere until you tell me the truth.

ZACK: Fine. You want the truth. Here's the truth …

> *The* ZOMBIES *pause to listen.*

I love you—but you are way too freaking intense.

SARAH: I'm committed.

ZACK: You're suffocating.

> ZOMBIES *attack again.*

CHRISTOPHER: Quickly, Blasko, time is running out.

PENELOPE: We have a specially engraved Magnum 45 just for you.

BLASKO: The guns will not work. I filled them with superglue. Oh—and I also stole your watches.

She holds up her arm—three watches.

PENELOPE: She filled our guns with superglue.

CHRISTOPHER: She stole our watches.

PENELOPE: Resourceful.

CHRISTOPHER: Inventive.

PENELOPE & CHRISTOPHER: [*together*] Extremely effective.

SARAH: Zack.

ZACK: [*taken by* ZOMBIES] Sarah!

BLASKO: [*hearing their cry*] Sarah? Zack?

SUCK-FACE: Motor-mouth!

BLASKO: Mother, father.

SARAH: [*hearing her voice*] Blasko?

BLASKO: Sarah.

PENELOPE & CHRISTOPHER: [*together*] Sarah?

SARAH: Blasko!

PENELOPE & CHRISTOPHER: [*together*] Blasko.

BLASKO *must choose.*

BLASKO: Bollywood diversion!

SCENE TEN

BLASKO *launches into a Bollywood routine. The* ZOMBIES *cannot resist the rhythm.* CHRISTOPHER *and* PENELOPE *escape with* MOTOR-MOUTH.

SONG: 'THE B.F.F. I NEVER HAD'

BLASKO: [*singing*] 'Don't want to overstate the situation
         Don't want to be a party pooper—no
         But I've done a quick and thorough calculation
         And the odds of us surviving this are low'

SARAH: 'Tell me something I don't know'

BLASKO: 'A hundred zombies growing by the minute'

SARAH: [*spoken*] I knew that too.

BLASKO: 'A hundred zombies baying for our blood'

SARAH: 'Think we'll make it to the next dimension?'

BLASKO: 'Maybe—either way my party's been a dud'
SARAH: 'It's been different'
BLASKO: 'Try disaster'
SARAH: 'The food was amazing'
BLASKO: 'You're just being nice—'
SARAH: 'No—I really mean it'
BLASKO: 'So nice to hear it'
SARAH: 'Don't feel too bad'
BLASKO: 'Sarah—'
SARAH: 'Yes—Blasko?'
BLASKO: 'You're the B.F.F.—I never had'
    [*Spoken*] That stands for—
SARAH: [*spoken*] Best friends forever, I know.
BLASKO: 'It's true—until tonight
             I only had my mum and dad
             You're the B.F.F.—I never had'
SARAH: 'You were right and I was wrong
             I should have listened
             Get out of here before they all attack
             I've been an idiot, I couldn't see the truth
             And to top it off I just broke up with Zack'
BLASKO: 'You just broke up?'
SARAH: 'Yes, we broke up'
BLASKO: 'How did he take it?'
SARAH: 'Eaten by zombies'
BLASKO: 'He took it bad then'
SARAH: [*spoken*] Yes—he took it bad!
BLASKO: 'A mutual break-up?'
SARAH: 'No, not exactly'
BLASKO: 'You did the breaking?'
SARAH: 'He did the breaking'
BLASKO: 'You must be sad, yes?'
SARAH: 'Can we discuss this later?'
BLASKO: 'I feel so bad that you feel sad because
             You're the B.F.F.—I never had'
SARAH: [*spoken*] Kill me now.
BLASKO: 'And if we're eaten by zombies
             I take the blame—it's my bad

Because you're the B.F.F.—I never had'

SUCK-FACE *sits on a diving board holding the brain and a trigger.*

SUCK-FACE: 'Should we or shouldn't we blow up?
            What else can we do?'

Light shifts. The wormhole begins to open.

BLASKO: 'Never had'

SARAH: 'I see—I see—I see the wormhole'

SUCK-FACE: 'With just a brain, will we make it?'
            Will we see it through?'

BLASKO: 'Never had'

SARAH: 'I see—I see—I see the wormhole'

SUCK-FACE: 'Wherever you're going, I'm going too'

SARAH: [*spoken*] For crying out loud, Blasko—*look!*

They all stare at the wormhole—while SUCK-FACE *sings to the brain.*

SONG: 'ICKY LOVE'

SUCK-FACE: [*singing*] 'Because … I love you
            I really love you
            It feels so weird to tell you
            But not because it's not true
            Just because it's icky
            Not icky in a bad way
            It's icky in the right way
            But hard for me to say it
            Because I really mean it
            And I'm sorry it's taken so long
            And I couldn't say the words to your face
            Or look you in the eye
            I don't know why—I guess I—
            Well, you know what it's like

            When you are ugly
            You think—how could he love me?
            It feels so bleh to want it
            Even though you really want it

I needed you to show me
I needed you to want me
And that was really stupid
I feel really, really stupid
I hope you can forgive me
And I hope you can hear without ears
And it's not too late to be telling you now
But I at least had to try
If this is our last goodbye
Then I—love you'
ZOMBIES: 'She really loves you'
SUCK-FACE: 'And saying it feels wonderful'
ZOMBIES: 'She loves you'
SUCK-FACE: 'Saying it's incredible'
ZOMBIES: 'She really loves you'
SUCK-FACE: 'Because I know you love me'
ZOMBIES: 'He really loves you'
SUCK-FACE: 'And I really love you'

> CHRISTOPHER *and* PENELOPE *sing to their daughter, waving goodbye.*

PENELOPE
& CHRISTOPHER: 'We really love you'
SUCK-FACE: 'I'm in love'
ALL: 'Love, love, love'

> ZOMBIE BOY *holds a clear balloon.* ZOMBIE HILARY *holds the polar bear.*

SUCK-FACE: 'I'm in love'
ALL: 'Love, love, love'
SUCK-FACE: 'I'm in love'
ALL: 'Love, love, love

> SUCK-FACE *detonates the bomb.* ZOMBIE BOY *pops the balloon. The sound of a loud explosion.* CHRISTOPHER *injures his hand as debris floats over the* ZOMBIES. BLASKO *and* SARAH *watch the wormhole in awe.*

Heart, be a radio'
PENELOPE

& CHRISTOPHER: 'You will hand over the gun'
ALL: 'Heart, be a radio'
PENELOPE
& CHRISTOPHER: 'You will hand over the gun'
ALL: 'Heart, be a radio'
PENELOPE
& CHRISTOPHER: 'You will hand over the gun'

> SARAH *is consumed by the* ZOMBIES. BLASKO *escapes.*

SCENE ELEVEN

CHRISTOPHER *and* PENELOPE *try to hypnotise the police officer.* MOTOR-MOUTH *struts, waving his anxiety extractor.* CHRISTOPHER*'s hand is bandaged.*

PENELOPE: I'm sorry, officer?
CHRISTOPHER: Who is this young man with the strange apparatus on his head?
PENELOPE: Oh—just some delirious boy from the party.
BLASKO: [*to the audience*] Shut up and listen.
CHRISTOPHER: You know how teenagers can be.
PENELOPE: Rebellious.
CHRISTOPHER: Irresponsible.
BLASKO: In exactly one minute and fifty-three seconds a solar flare will strike the earth.
PENELOPE: Why, now that I think about it, he could be very dangerous.
CHRISTOPHER: Completely deranged.
BLASKO: Setting off a chain reaction incinerating every living creature on the face of the planet.
PENELOPE: You should take out your weapon.
CHRISTOPHER: While there's still time.
PENELOPE: Speaking of time …
BLASKO: My name is Blasko Tupper—prepare to die.

> BLASKO *inflates a large balloon rendered like the earth.*

SONG: 'HAND OVER THE GUN'—REPRISE

PENELOPE: [*singing*] 'Wait! Is that the time?'

CHRISTOPHER: 'The time?'
PENELOPE: 'Yes—Eastern Standard Time'
CHRISTOPHER: 'My watch is gone'
PENELOPE: 'Our daughter stole them'
CHRISTOPHER: 'Officer?'
PENELOPE: 'You said the time was—'
CHRISTOPHER: 'That's the time?'
PENELOPE: 'Oh dear, it's late'
CHRISTOPHER: 'It's very late'
PENELOPE: 'We should be going'
CHRISTOPHER: 'Very late!'
PENELOPE: 'We shouldn't keep you from the—'
CHRISTOPHER: 'Bodies!'
PENELOPE: 'Lots of—'
CHRISTOPHER: 'Bodies!'
PENELOPE: 'Well, goodbye, been so much fun'
CHRISTOPHER: 'Before we go'
PENELOPE: 'We have to run'
CHRISTOPHER: 'Give us the gun'
PENELOPE: 'Been so much fun'
CHRISTOPHER: 'Before we're done'
PENELOPE: 'The freaking gun!'
BOTH: 'You must hand over the gun'
CHRISTOPHER: 'You will—'
PENELOPE: 'Look into my eyes'
CHRISTOPHER: 'You will—'
PENELOPE: 'Look into my eyes'
CHRISTOPHER: 'You will'
ZOMBIES: 'Five'
BOTH: 'Hand over the—'
ZOMBIES: 'Four'
BOTH: 'Hand over the—'
ZOMBIES: 'Three'
BOTH: 'Hand over the—'
ZOMBIES: 'Two, one'

    BLASKO *holds a huge needle—poised to plunge into the balloon.*

CHRISTOPHER: [*spoken*] *Sacrebleu!*

PENELOPE: Oh, shit.

> BLASKO *plunges the needle.*
>
> *Blackout, followed by a huge explosion.*

SCENE TWELVE

Inside the cosmic wormhole. MOTOR-MOUTH'S CONSCIOUSNESS *is floating.*

MOTOR-MOUTH: Hello? Is anybody there? Suck-face, if you can hear me, I love you too. Wait a minute. What am I saying? She can't hear me—she has no ears. Come to think of it—how am I speaking if I have no mouth? A consciousness can only think. I must be thinking out loud. But am I thinking loud enough out loud? Maybe I should try thinking out loud, even louder.

> SUCK-FACE'S CONSCIOUSNESS *is floating in space.*

SUCK-FACE: Motor-mouth?

MOTOR-MOUTH: Suck-face? Is that you?

SUCK-FACE: Wow. So this is a cosmic wormhole.

MOTOR-MOUTH: I can't see you. Can you see me?

SUCK-FACE: No—but I can hear you. Oh, and I can … feel you.

MOTOR-MOUTH: Oooo—that's probably our atomic particles in close proximity.

SUCK-FACE: Very close proximity.

MOTOR-MOUTH: You may also experience a little dizziness.

SUCK-FACE: For someone who just exploded I feel pretty good.

MOTOR-MOUTH: Actually, now that you mention it, my senses also seem heightened by our current state of existence.

SUCK-FACE: How long will it take to reach the next dimension?

MOTOR-MOUTH: I estimate a travel of time of approximately ten minutes.

SUCK-FACE: Hmm. Ten whole minutes. Alone in the dark. Just the two of us.

MOTOR-MOUTH: Are you thinking what I'm thinking or is that me thinking what I'm thinking?

SUCK-FACE: Are you feeling what I'm feeling?

MOTOR-MOUTH: I'm feeling the need for ice cubes and constant therapeutic masturbation.

SUCK-FACE: Oh, Motor-mouth.

MOTOR-MOUTH: Oh, Suck-face.

BOTH: Oh, oh, oh—

MOTOR-MOUTH: No, no, no, stop—stop—stop. We're forgetting something.

SUCK-FACE: Do they make condoms for cosmic wormholes?

MOTOR-MOUTH: Professor Pluto!

SUCK-FACE: Professor Pluto?

PROFESSOR PLUTO'S CONSCIOUSNESS *appears.*

MOTOR-MOUTH: Professor Pluto. Avert your consciousness immediately.

PROFESSOR PLUTO'S CONSCIOUSNESS *disappears.*

SUCK-FACE: Has he gone?

MOTOR-MOUTH: I think so. Maybe we should wait—Oh, oh—or maybe not—

BOTH: Oh. Oh, oh, oh, oh, oh, *oh!*

The sounds of sex crescendo.

SCENE THIRTEEN

Schoolyard. The other dimension. Lights up on TIFFANY, TANK, HUGO, ZACK, SARAH, HILARY *and* ZOMBIE BOY—*now a normal boy—holding a meeting of the 'Save The World' club. The same—but different.*

TIFFANY: Quiet! Firstly, let me take this opportunity to, like, thank everyone for their *tra-mun-dous* efforts on the fundraising triathlon last weekend. The good news is we raised—

ZACK: Three hundred and forty-two dollars.

TIFFANY: Which goes towards our charity of the month—

SARAH: Greenpeace.

ZACK: And still leaves enough to buy a present for Professor Pluto—

TIFFANY: Who, like, just won the bathtub race *and*—

SARAH: The Nobel Peace Prize for saving the planet with his revolutionary solar panel.

Applause.

HUGO: Yeah. No. Wait. We almost burned to death?

HILARY: If Professor Pluto hadn't invented his solar panel.

TIFFANY: If Motor-mouth hadn't superglued the plug in his bathtub.

HILARY: Everything on the planet would cease to exist.

SARAH: Except radio waves.

TANK: Radio waves travel through space and time—da.

HUGO: Whoa, man—Elvis singing 'Hound Dog' for eternity.

TANK: Kylie Minogue—'Fever'.

SARAH: Maria Carey—'We Belong Together'.

ZACK: Queen—'I Want To Break Free'.

TIFFANY: Gwen Stefani—'Rich Girl'.

HILARY: Whitney Houston—'I Will Always Love You'.

ZOMBIE BOY: The Cranberries—'Zombie'.

> MOTOR-MOUTH *and* SUCK-FACE *brandish a chainsaw and power drill.*

SUCK-FACE: Lady Gaga—'Edge of Glory'.

MOTOR-MOUTH: Lionel Ritchie—'All Night Long'.

SUCK-FACE: But that's not important right now.

MOTOR-MOUTH: What's important is this.

SUCK-FACE: Because if you can understand this—

> BLASKO *enters with her chainsaw.*

BLASKO: If by some miracle, clarity wedges its sweet toe through the dark door of apathy …

SUCK-FACE: Then maybe—just maybe there's hope for us all …

MOTOR-MOUTH: In this knee-deep, existential sludge-pile we so loosely refer to as life.

BLASKO: Translation?

SONG: 'IN THE OTHER DIMENSION'

SUCK-FACE: [*singing*] 'In the other dimension
                   Gonna feel our heat'

MOTOR-MOUTH: 'In the other dimension
                   Hold onto your seat—we're in'

BOTH: 'Love, baby, and we're'

ALL: 'On our way to seize the day
                   In the other dimension'

TANK: 'In the other dimension
                   We'll save the polar bear'

TIFFANY: 'In the other dimension
                  We'll change the world with some flair'
BLASKO: 'In the other dimension
                  Gonna lock and load'
SARAH: 'In the other dimension
                  Time to hit the road and save the'
ALL: 'World, baby—jump aboard the train'
HILARY: 'No-one eats our brain'
ALL: 'In the other dimension'
SARAH, ZACK,
TANK & HUGO: 'Love gets a second chance
                  In the other dimension'
ALL: 'We all get a second chance with some
                  Global warming, cosmic intervention
                  In the other dimension'
HUGO: 'We're gonna start a band'
ZACK: 'In the other dimension
                  We're gonna make our stand'
ZOMBIE BOY
& HILARY: 'In the other dimension
                  Solar panels rock'
MOTOR-MOUTH: 'Come take a ride through a wormhole'
MOTOR-MOUTH
& SUCK-FACE: 'You don't have to knock, baby, we're'
ALL: 'All dying together
                  So hold my hand and let's elope
                  To where there's hope
                  In the other dimension
                  In the other dimension
                  In the other dimension!'

THE END

www.ingramcontent.com/pod-product-compliance
Lightning Source LLC
Chambersburg PA
CBHW050018090426
42734CB00021B/3326